Black Smoke

Black Smoke

A Woman's Journey of Healing,
Wild Love, and Transformation
in the Amazon

MARGARET DE WYS

STERLING

New York / London
www.sterlingpublishing.com

STERLING and the distinctive Sterling logo are registered trademarks of
Sterling Publishing Co., Inc.

Library of Congress Cataloging-in-Publication Data

De Wys, Margaret.
 Black smoke : a woman's journey of healing, wild love, and transformation in
the Amazon / Margaret De Wys.
   p. cm.
 ISBN 978-1-4027-4883-7
 1. De Wys, Margaret. 2. Breast--Cancer--Patients--Biography. 3. Shamans--
Ecuador. I. Title.
 RC280.B8D387 2008
 362.196'994490092--dc22
 [B]
                                        2008024988

10 9 8 7 6 5 4 3 2 1

Published by Sterling Publishing Co., Inc.
387 Park Avenue South, New York, NY 10016
© 2009 by Margaret De Wys
Distributed in Canada by Sterling Publishing
c/o Canadian Manda Group, 165 Dufferin Street
Toronto, Ontario, Canada M6K 3H6
Distributed in the United Kingdom by GMC Distribution Services
Castle Place, 166 High Street, Lewes, East Sussex, England BN7 1XU
Distributed in Australia by Capricorn Link (Australia) Pty. Ltd.
P.O. Box 704, Windsor, NSW 2756, Australia

Sterling ISBN 978-1-4027-4883-7

For information about custom editions, special sales, premium and
corporate purchases, please contact Sterling Special Sales
Department at 800-805-5489 or specialsales@sterlingpublishing.com.

This book is for Manon and Mike

AUTHOR'S NOTE

Although the story I am telling is true, names and places have been
changed to protect people in Ecuador, the United States, and
Canada. For the sake of the story line, I have condensed serveral
time periods. Between 2000 and 2003 I made eleven trips to South
America. Each stay was approximately one month long.

Contents

PART ONE

INITIATION

CHAPTER ONE

Gum Boots

I arrived at Mariscal Sucre Airport in Quito, the capital of Ecuador, in the middle of the night. My body, unaccustomed to the altitude of nine thousand feet, felt heavy and slow, but there was also a nervous energy about me, an aura of excitement and dread.

Despite the late hour, the terminal was full of Ecuadorian Indians who had bribed their way or otherwise insinuated themselves into the no-man's-land between customs and the real world. They shouted and waved at me, grabbing at my bag, begging for money, offering me rides and places to stay. I felt like darting back into the terminal's more privileged recesses and taking the first plane home. Then I spotted Carlos's round face in the chaos of the crowd. He was the reason I had left my home and family to come on an adventure that most of my friends—professional, middle-aged New Yorkers—had looked at askance. "You're going *where*, to do *what*?" they said. "Isn't that a little bit *extreme*?"

Carlos, a Shuar *uwishin* from the Ecuadorian jungles of the Upper Amazon, had launched me on this journey several months earlier. In the culture of the indigenous Shuar people, the uwishin fills the role of a medical doctor, practices magic, and acts as an intercessor between man and the divine. In February of 2000 I had met Carlos at the Mayan ruins of Tikal, Guatemala, where I had traveled to participate in a gathering of indigenous American healers. Dozens of Native Americans had come from as far away as the northern Canadian Rockies and Tierra del Fuego down to the southern parts of Chile to participate in the Mayan ceremony for the New Year. Carlos was standing between immense steles on the top of the Temple of Masks, singing in a language that I'd never heard. He was bare-chested, with cinnamon skin, almond eyes, and a compact muscular body. He wore a brightly colored corona of red and gold toucan feathers and a bandolier of seeds that vibrated softly, like the tail of a waking rattlesnake, when he moved. To say that he was charismatic doesn't begin to describe his power.

In Guatemala, in a ceremony with about a dozen other visitors, Carlos initiated me into *la medicina sagrada* (sacred medicine). Central to Carlos's practices—and general traditional shamanic practice in the Upper Amazon—is the use of ayahuasca, an extract made from native jungle plants known to cause visions. Carlos brewed the vine by mixing it with other medicinal plants. It was the medium through which he practiced his vision, clairvoyance, and healing.

"I can see inside your body," Carlos said during that first ayahuasca journey. "Your body is transparent, like a drinking glass. The ayahuasca and 'doctor' spirits have shown me where to heal you. Black smoke is trapped in your breast."

No one in Guatemala knew I was sick with breast cancer—that I had come there purposely to find someone to help me.

"How can you see these things?" I asked.

"I 'see' with my spiritual eyes. I can enter the veins and organs of the infirm. I see also that you are blind in your left eye. I don't know if I can assist you with that. It appears to be an old illness. But, if you wish, I will attempt it."

I noticed the elegance of his Spanish, although I didn't know at the time that he had been taken in by Silesian priests as a child and trained for the clergy. I learned that he came from the tribes of the Jivaro, which only a generation ago had been shrinking heads and hunting with curare-tipped darts. He worked with me for three days while the gathering of healers continued.

"Margarita, your healing is not complete," said Carlos, before I was due to return to the United States. "You need more treatments. You must come to Ecuador. There we can work together to finish the healing that we have begun."

"Are you sure you're thinking clearly?" my husband had said as I prepared for my second trip. "I can't understand this single-mindedness of yours, and why you think this is going to work." In the middle of the night in a strange country, about to entrust my life and health to a man I barely knew who had grown up hunting with poisoned darts and warring neighboring jungle tribes, I suddenly felt that he might be right.

I'd made a strong decision, right or wrong. I gathered my courage and told myself there was no turning back. I pushed my way toward Carlos. He barely greeted me, grabbing my arm instead and pulling me through the shouting, imploring crowd. Outside the airport, scavengers looked on, surly and dangerous in the dim lights of the streets. Quito was dark and filthy, its buildings shuttered and peeling.

I was distressed to see that Carlos looked nothing like he had in Guatemala. There, he had been regal, dressed in ceremonial costume and the gorgeous feather headdress that designated him an uwishin. In Quito, I barely recognized him. His face looked thicker than it had on our last meeting, and he wore cheap Western clothes. He was just an average man, with none of the charisma that had so impressed me in Guatemala.

Carlos ushered me into a waiting car, introducing me to his son

Mauro and two other Ecuadorians—wild-looking men with long hair and mustaches who grinned and gawked and couldn't seem to take their black eyes off my long blond hair. It flashed through my mind that I could be raped and robbed and left for dead.

I sat in the backseat next to Carlos. My scattered thoughts kept coming back to an acute anxiety about my safety and an awareness of just how vulnerable I was. My face was stiff, and I couldn't catch my breath. Not a squeak escaped my lips. I sat there, mute and trembling.

"I am taking you to a quiet place," Carlos said, "in the mountains outside the city where you can sleep." The cadence of his Spanish was soothing, hypnotic, and, almost magically, I felt my breath return and my face relax.

Carlos seemed distracted, or perhaps just private, as we drove out of the city. He might have been tired; I don't know. He just quit speaking. Eventually we came to a locked iron gate. A night watchman appeared, lumbering forward on bowed legs, and opened the gate. Carlos led me to a ground-floor room and handed me the key.

"We leave in the early morning for the jungle. Be ready at five."

I looked at my watch. It was 2:00 A.M. I was completely disoriented and needed some kind of reassurance.

"Are you going to begin the healing in the jungle?" I asked.

"Yes, Margarita. Do not worry," Carlos said. "I have made all the preparations."

Carlos turned and walked back to the car, whistling. I didn't know it at the time, but when Carlos whistled, it was *always* to call the spirits.

When Carlos came for me the next morning, I was shivering; the air was chilly and thin, and I hadn't packed for it, thinking that Ecuador was equatorial and therefore warm. In the early light I saw that the inn stood on a mountaintop, a vast Andean panorama surrounding it, undisturbed but for birdsong.

Carlos, dressed exactly as before, looked haggard. It seemed that he hadn't slept. After leaving me, he had witnessed a hit and run. "The victim," he said as we drove, "was in shock, with a big wound in his chest. I stopped the bleeding, bandaged his head, and put my hands on him to reduce the swelling."

"Carlos saved the man," added Jorge, the driver and owner of the car. "When he was stabilized, we drove him home."

I recalled that Carlos had spontaneously healed a local woman in Guatemala. He wrapped his hands around her head, squeezed and massaged her temples, and blew into the top of her skull. She smiled and declared that her headache was gone.

On that same trip, I saw Carlos help a man who had badly twisted his ankle. Tears fell from the man's eyes when Carlos worked on his foot. Several minutes into the impromptu healing, the man stood up, thanked Carlos profusely, and went on his way.

I mentioned these incidents to Carlos as we wound our way down the mountain. "How can you heal people with your hands?" I asked.

"I am a channel for healing energy," he said. "Sometimes when you would see me in Guatemala I had to cover my mouth because the energy is so strong that I have to regulate its flow into others whom I am healing. I take the power of this healing energy and put it inside the sick person. This energy is called *Shunta Sinsa*, a living force that the elders have given those of us who have been initiated as master healers, which we in turn give to the sick person."

"Is that how you intend to help me?"

Carlos didn't reply.

At dawn Jorge dropped us at the bus station where, it seemed, all of Ecuador had decided to assemble. The derelict station, swarming with people, stood in sharp contrast to the exclusivity of the airport. We met up with Carlos's son Mauro and a small group of Indians who Carlos said would accompany us into the jungle.

Mauro was small-boned, perhaps 5' 9", with incredibly thick, silky, straight black hair. He was dark-skinned with chiseled lips and Carlos's upward-slanting almond eyes.

The sign on the brow of the fuming, shaking bus we boarded said PUYO. I climbed aboard and sat wedged between Carlos and the window. His body was compact, hard, and pressed in on me. I felt swaddled and cramped and slightly unnerved by such close proximity.

The city with its crowds and heavy traffic was soon behind us. We were on the open road, but we traveled slowly in a line of buses and trucks. Carlos directed my attention to the landscape. Quito was ringed by active volcanoes, which rose in giant cones out of the upland valleys and smoldered at their tops.

We journeyed down the Andes' eastern face. The bus swayed around the curves, precariously suspended over deep gorges. Looking down, I could see thin footbridges slung over raging rivers. It was fascinating and horrible. Vehicles edged past one another on the narrow muddy road. There were no guardrails. Carlos pointed to a giant crevice clogged with mud. "Two weeks ago a bus tumbled to the bottom of the canyon. There were no survivors," he said.

"Does that happen often?" I asked.

"Every couple of months. Some bus drivers don't pay attention to the roads." Our driver had a cross dangling from the rearview mirror, and statues and amulets on the dashboard—items that I would see on every bus that traveled the Andes. "Don't worry," Carlos continued. "Before I get on a bus, I look at the driver. I can *see* if he will have an accident. This driver is good. You will always be under my protection when you are with me."

Under my protection? I chafed a bit at the overt chauvinism. But the fact was that I *did* need protection. Could I believe in his prescience—what to my ear smacked of the supernatural? And if I didn't believe in him and his abilities, which were so completely different from those of my doctors in New York, then what was I doing here? I'd already investigated alternative cancer treatments offered in Europe, Mexico, and the Caribbean. Even though the protocols appeared to have favorable success rates, the treatments were illegal in the United States.

I looked at him, feeling shy, wanting to say something. "I don't think you know how different your country is from mine, how differently we think. In my world, people who claim to see the future are dismissed as lunatics."

Carlos laughed. "Do you think the seeds of the future are contained in the present?"

"Of course. But the way the future forms is immensely complicated and difficult to see."

"Maybe not as difficult as you think. It depends on how we 'see.'"

"Carlos," I said, quavering a bit, "I hope your kind of healing works for me. I am nervous, and yet I feel as if something important is going to take place and my life will change. In what way, I don't know. I am so afraid of the smoke, of what's inside me."

I must have looked ghastly, because he put his hand on my arm and looked at me with great gravity and tenderness. "Do not think of that now," he said, and his voice had the same soothing hypnotic quality of the night before. "Healing is holy, Margarita," he said, almost chanting. "Healing is beauty. Healing is simplicity. It is purity. But it is also very serious business! You have to participate completely. There will be no holding back, and it won't be easy. You will have to fight to regain your health. These are very serious challenges, Margarita. I know it is probably hard for you to accept this, but you were meant to come to the Amazon. It is written in the stars in the same way as the safety of this journey. You have come. You made the first step. You trusted your instincts. That is important, and I will watch over you. But ultimately, these things are in the hands of the Great Spirit."

I didn't know what to think of all this, but there was one thing that was clear to me: Carlos was absolutely sincere.

There were no toilets on the bus, and I soon got antsy, squirming in my seat. "Carlos, is this bus going to stop somewhere soon?"

"It continues straight on to Puyo. It will stop there."

Late in the afternoon, the country leveled out. We passed through a military checkpoint. *Thank God,* I thought. *Finally I can pee!* I was getting off the bus when two machine-gun-toting soldiers confronted me.

"Passport," said one. He flipped through it quickly. "Come with us," he said.

Carlos rose to accompany me, although I could sense his uneasiness.

"Sit down," the soldier commanded, and Carlos, rather compliantly I thought, obeyed.

I was brought to a checkpoint booth. The *capitán*, an unpleasant military type, grilled me, patting his holster now and then. Why was I going into the jungle? What was my purpose? How long did I intend to stay? What was I carrying on me? He acted as if I would be conducting criminal activity. The other soldiers spoke rapidly, accusingly. Three men stood close behind me, as if I was going to make a run for it! I would learn that because of the sensitive politics of the region, and because I was clearly not Ecuadorian Spanish or indigenous, I would be questioned by the military each time I crossed a jungle frontier.

Finally, they were done, and I headed gratefully for the outhouse. But it was not to be. "Hurry, hurry," Carlos called. "The bus is leaving without you!"

We finally arrived in Puyo, a sizable frontier town of mud streets lined with dilapidated wood and cinderblock buildings, many of which were painted in colors that had weathered from bright to tawdry. The horizon was dotted with oil rigs. Music blared from the doorways of the cantinas, which were everywhere, and the town smelled of quick money, quick sex, and booze.

At the outdoor market, we picked up vegetables, yucca, plantains, bananas, mangos, limes, and grains. We bought live chickens, which were packed in a burlap bag with holes in it for their heads to stick out. I ate *ayampaco*, a sort of Shuar tamale with vegetables, greens, chicken, palm, and snails all wrapped in plantain leaves and fire roasted. I had not eaten since the plane, and I was famished.

I checked the crowds for Carlos. I had given him cash to pay for all the expenses we would incur before we set out for the Amazon, and he ran around pinching vegetables and haggling with marketers over prices. He was barking orders at everyone. "Get this. Get that. Hurry!" He was coming back into recognizable form. He was in control, more in his element, more and more the charismatic man who had riveted me in Guatemala.

He sauntered over to me holding a sheaf of herbs, their nappy buds bobbing like miniature pom-poms, and presented it to me as if it were a bouquet. "Margarita, *quieres manzanilla?*" he asked.

The flowers smelled so good and fresh. I bowed my head in assent. "Yes, Carlos. I'd love some chamomile."

Our supplies were packed into large red and white plastic sacks, and we loaded everything into the truck Jorge had arranged with a driver from Puyo and drove off. As soon as we left the main street of Puyo, the jungle closed in. We bumped along a narrow pitted track, ropy with roots. The vegetation was so thick that we didn't see the sun disappear. Suddenly it was dark.

We pitched and heaved through the night. Carlos was in a boisterous mood and often broke into song. The men laughed at his jokes. He seemed to be drawing energy from the jungle around us. The road narrowed still more. Our headlights illuminated little more than vines and branches scraping against the truck's sides. We kept going, going, going—pushing the truck's blunt nose forward until there was no more road. Only then did we disembark. Insects rasped. The air smelled as if I had stuck my nose in the bowl of a potted plant, full of nutrients and dirt. The dense canopy allowed no starlight through. The darkness was weighty, like a cave.

Carlos pulled a pair of rubber boots from one of his suitcases and handed them to me.

"Put these on."

"Right now?"

He gave me the eye. I unlaced my hiking boots.

"Take off your socks."

"Thanks, I'll leave them on."

"You must take off your socks in the jungle. You must learn to grip with your toes like a monkey. You *will* learn how to walk in the jungle."

I removed my socks and put them and my heavy leather boots in my backpack. The rubber boots were two sizes too big. Their soles were purposely thin. Okay, I thought. No big deal.

"*Tienes una lampara?*" Carlos asked. No one had purchased flashlights in Quito, but I had two small lights in my backpack and handed him one.

"Is it possible to carry all this equipment?" I asked, astonished.

"Warriors can carry much more than this," he said. "Soon you will be a warrior too!" I started with alarm. "But for now you will take care of your own backpack, and we will handle the rest."

We started down a steep grade. All at once it was pouring, and I was instantly drenched. Then the downpour stopped as suddenly as it had begun. Everything dripped. The air was so full of vegetable smells that it was like breathing in salad. Carlos had said I would become a warrior. What did he mean? I just wanted to get well.

The Indians moved gracefully under their enormous burdens. Some were barefoot. Their feet were their eyes. Everything moved congenially for them. Their bodies, breathtakingly attuned to the land, conversed fluently with the murderous slopes. They moved silently. When they weren't joking with one another, they disappeared into the night, incorporated into the dark foliage.

Then chaos erupted. Carlos called out the names of everyone in the group only to find one member missing. He shouted in panic and ran back along the trail. The Indians talked fast in their native tongue, and I stood frozen, unsure what to do. One of the men stepped forward, indicating that I should follow him.

"Where's Carlos?" I asked.

"He's meeting us later," the Indian replied.

"Where has he gone?"

"Don't worry. Follow me. I know the way to the village."

"I don't want to do that!" I cried.

My last bit of composure vanished. Now I was walking through the jungle with men whose names I didn't know or couldn't remember. I hadn't spoken two words to Mauro; he'd kept his distance from me and Carlos. I wanted to call out and curse Carlos for disappearing. What was so important that he had run off? Shouldn't I run too? But where would I go? I trudged on warily.

The path forked, and I shuffled to a stop. "*Ven. Ven,*" cried the man in front of me. "Come. Come."

Then I saw lights, which, as we got closer, I could see were torches. Carlos was there, talking animatedly with a small group of people in front of palm-thatched dwellings.

"Carlos, how did you get here?" I asked him. "Why did you run off like that?"

"My friend here," he pointed to the man next to him, "had taken another path. But I didn't know that. I ran to make sure that the crocodiles that live on the banks of the lagoons hadn't attacked him. When I found him, we both decided to take a shortcut to the village."

I looked at him with what must have been a mixture of frustration, anger, and relief. He smiled like an imp.

About twenty Shuar and Quechua lived in the village, all part of a large extended family. Jorge, the patriarch, greeted us. He was lean and tough with parched brown skin and black eyes that gleamed in the torchlight. He exuded a carnal, unrepentant masculinity. He wore a necklace of jaguar teeth and monkey heads. One of his hands had been partially bitten off by a crocodile. He ran his eyes over my body, face, and hair in a way that suggested he might be wondering if I'd make a good conquest. *"Bienvenido a mi casa,"* he said and introduced me to his wife, known simply as *Tia*, who was Carlos's aunt.

Jorge spoke in rapid Quechua to one of the men, who snapped into action and took my backpack. I felt as if I could float upward when it was removed from my shoulders. My hair was matted to my head. My clothes were filthy. Jorge leered. But frankly, I couldn't have cared less. What a day it had been! I turned away from Jorge and smiled at the villagers, which I could see registered a good impression.

The food and equipment we had brought from Puyo quickly disappeared. "Mauro is going to take you to your sleeping quarters now," said Carlos.

In the torchlight I could see a fine, barely visible mustache on Mauro's upper lip. I wondered why he had kept his distance from us. Perhaps he was afraid of his father? Or perhaps he was just shy around the gringa from the north? His inky black hair was slicked back into a ponytail. I could see that he, too, was tired, but he gave me his friendliest smile. Although he was just eighteen, I knew from our journey to the village that he was impossibly strong. His sinuous muscles, like those of the other Indians, had developed from hard work, not trips to the gym.

Mauro held a small white candle in his hand, and I followed him to a large thatched-roofed structure on stilts and up rough stairs that led to a sleeping area arranged with ten beds. He lit another candle so that I could see in the room, told me where the outhouse was, and then left me. The beds were more like small cots—narrow, truncated children's beds made of planks with thin mattresses and mosquito netting. I chose the one next to an open window. But before I let down the netting, something crawly dropped onto my head from the thatch. I squealed and shook violently. It was big, whatever it was—a grotesque, crawling, skittering thing. I stared suspiciously at the bed with the candle in my hand, inspecting it inch by inch. I didn't want to lie down on a spider or something worse. I considered the possibility that a snake lay in the palm thatch above me.

Although I was exhausted, I was too wound up to sleep much. Lying on the hard cot, I thought of my husband and my daughter and the college in upstate New York where I taught music. I particularly missed my daughter, who was fifteen, and I remembered her pleading eyes when I told her I was going into the jungle. I had kept from her just how sick I was, that my life was in danger, but somehow I think she knew, and she couldn't understand why I was going away, why being with her and her father was not what I had chosen to do.

With my husband, that sense of incomprehension and hurt was just as visceral but more thought through. "Why do you have to go?" he asked. "Why don't you want to do what your very able doctors here recommend? They're the experts. You're not alone in this!"

It breaks my heart to remember his words. In retrospect, I realize how completely isolated I felt, unable to respond to the ways in which the people I loved reached out for me. But the truth was that they could only reach so far. The existential loneliness I felt was crushing. I was cornered. I couldn't breathe. I hated and feared the thing inside me, and I hated myself. I needed to scream or wail but I went numb instead—and deep inside I knew that numbness was going to be the end of me.

Healing is beauty. Healing is simplicity. It is purity, Carlos had said. I repeated those words over and over again throughout the night—a refrain, a mantra. *You have come. Made the first step. Trusted your instincts.*

CHAPTER TWO

Purging

My eyes popped open as it was getting light. Everyone in the room, including Carlos and all the other members of our group, still slept. But I was eager to get the lay of the land, so I slipped into my rubber boots and down the stairs.

The light was coming up fast. Birds were singing; below me was the river, wide as a lake and black against the greenery. Men were bathing naked, close to the bank. When they emerged from the water and returned to the huts, I walked down to the river's edge and splashed water on my face and neck. I was shocked to find that it was ice-cold. The jungle had already begun to heat up and become steamy, but the river had been born in the Andes and was as cold as melting snow.

As I made my way back to the huts, I met Carlos. He was energized. "Today you will become acclimatized and then tomorrow the healing will begin," he decreed. I was eager to get started and wanted to press him for details, but I held my tongue.

We entered a shedlike kitchen. Guinea pigs poked around on the dirt floor, tame and unafraid, sharing the kitchen with emaciated cats, which were much more skittish and furtive.

I am a cat lover, and I asked Carlos about this odd contrast. "The Shuar hate cats because of their *energía negativa*," he said. "The people here let them starve or be eaten by predators."

"What about the guinea pigs?" I asked. "They're fat with shiny coats."

"Yes. They are well cared for," he said. "They are supper."

A shudder ran through me at the thought of eating a rodent, but I would learn that they were actually quite tasty.

There was no refrigeration. A lone lightbulb hung over the center of the room, powered by a generator that was rarely used. The stove was a big wash pan with burning logs in it and a grate on top. Tia was preparing breakfast, boiling plantains, yucca, and herbal tea from the forest. These were the staples of the Shuar diet. No salt. No oil. Food was boiled in water and served.

Like all the village women, Tia was small, perhaps only five feet in height. She was dressed in an oversized man's T-shirt and gum boots. Her body was solid, almost stocky; her breasts were flat and widely spaced. I guessed she was in her fifties, although it was hard to tell her age. The thick black silk of her hair flowed down her back. Her teeth, like all the villagers', were brilliant—even, and gleaming white.

I ate from a wooden bowl with a metal spoon. Both the yucca and plantains were pasty, starchy, and faintly sweet. They were strong and easily digestible nourishment. The tea was full of tannin and spice.

I wanted to help Tia with the dishes, but she waved me away.

Carlos told Mauro to go with the men who would be cutting palm for roof patching. Then he turned to me. "Come," he said. "Let me show you the jungle."

In the brief time it had taken to eat breakfast, the morning had grown hot. Outside the small open area of the village we were immediately swallowed in foliage. The canopy of treetops towered high overhead, hung with vines that draped down to an understory of palmlike plants with huge fronds. Birds called, but in all the lush profusion there was a sense of solitude and stillness. We walked along a path that ran parallel to the river, and below me, to my right, I caught glimpses of the wide black body of swiftly moving water through the kaleidoscopic green.

"I've noticed that all the people in the village have perfect teeth. How is that possible, Carlos?" I asked. "I assume no one here goes to the dentist."

"That is certainly true," he replied. "Most of the *indigenas* have never even heard of a dentist. Please wait here, Margarita."

He went briefly off the path into the trees and came back holding a small plant, which he stripped of leaves. "This is what we use for brushing teeth," he said. "We chew it and rub it against our gums."

He handed it to me. "Please, Margarita. You must try it."

Again I felt myself rear back a little. He commanded rather than suggested and there was a dictatorial edge in his tone. Nonetheless, I chewed a bit on the fibrous stalk, which tasted slightly bitter and soapy but not unpleasant. And lo and behold: It made my teeth feel really fantastic.

We cut back into the jungle, away from the river, and the path dropped and joined another trail, snaking through the trees.

"This is the way we came last night," Carlos said. I was having trouble descending in my rubber boots and I had to constantly remind myself to grip the ground with my toes like a monkey.

The path leveled out and Carlos stopped. "These are the *lagunas*," he said. There were only clumps of trees here, hummocky islands in brackish water. My eyes widened in alarm. Crocodiles lounged on the islands' banks, and many more were half-submerged. The crocs, more than ten feet in length, didn't lunge at us as we passed, but the mere thought that they might unnerved me.

Soon we were climbing again. We approached a hidden waterfall and as I watched it tumble through the forest I felt myself fall under the spell of the place. Broad leaves steamed and the colors of wild-flowers flashed through the green. We were in an area so thickly vegetated that it felt subterranean. The treetop canopy was the surface of the earth and we lived beneath it, small creatures wending our way through the emerald caverns of extravagant growth, the twisting passageways of loam.

The terrain angled upward again in a wall of earth and roots. I was having a difficult time of it, slipping often. "Change the angle of your feet, center and approach the rise sideways," Carlos said. He took my hand in a sure, strong grip. "Sense the sureness of your foot before you give your weight to it. Slowly, Margarita."

Soon we came to a plateau. At its edge, the forest opened. Carlos pointed: "Over there is the Puyo River. Can you see where it meets the Pastaza River?"

"Water seems to be rushing in from so many directions. Where are you pointing? I don't see it."

"Do you see where the water is turbulent and angry? The rivers clash at this juncture. If you are on the water, it is very dangerous. Look there," he commanded, but this time I didn't mind his tone.

Vast floodplains spread beyond the river's banks. Farther off was an ocean of solid jungle rolling far into the distance. White water churned on the river. The view was wild and magnificent. The sky opened and rain cascaded over us, drenching everything. The storm abruptly ceased and mists rose. I was soaking wet, but I didn't care. The air was warm, and my pores were open.

That night I slept like a baby. The next morning my healing began.

"Margarita, today you will start cleansing," Carlos said. "This is a very important element in your healing."

He dipped a large cup into an old wooden barrel next to a flimsy shed and handed it to me. "Drink this quickly."

"What is it?"

"*Guayusa.*" Later I would learn that the botanical name for guayusa is *Piper callosum* from the plant family *Piperaceae*, of which there are more than 1,200 species in the Amazon basin. It is an emetic the Shuar use on a regular basis for digestive cleaning. It is supposedly a tonic to fight laziness, to help women become pregnant, and to promote successful hunting. But at the time I didn't know what I was holding.

A group of men from the village, who had already drunk the guayusa, were milling around. Suddenly they began vomiting. The liquid spewed out of them at high velocity, as if propelled by compressed gas. It was surreal, watching a semicircle of men repeatedly puke. I couldn't comprehend what I saw. Why were they throwing up?

Carlos stared at me expectantly. "Drink. It is time for you to vomit."

I couldn't have been more appalled. "What? Are you crazy? I'm not going to do that!"

"You *must* vomit in order to heal yourself."

"Any healing that requires me to vomit on demand is just not going to happen."

Carlos glared at me. "We are not moving from this spot until you vomit and keep vomiting!"

"You are a demon, Carlos. You can't force me to do this disgusting thing." I looked over at Mauro, who stood with the village men. My eyes pleaded with him to intercede on my behalf, but he shrugged as if to say that he could do nothing for me.

"You must vomit," Carlos repeated over and over. He was angry and unyielding.

"I'm leaving," I said. I don't know where I thought I was going. At any rate, Carlos was having none of it. He stood blocking my path, staring at me with a steely, unyielding fury. The entire male community was watching the showdown. It wasn't hard to imagine what they were thinking: *What a prima donna gringa!*

I took the cup from his hands and sipped the pale tea. It was slightly warm and tasted fine. I even *liked* it. I didn't let those impressions register on my face, but I cautiously sipped again.

"*No!*" Carlos shouted. "You must drink *quickly*. At least eleven cups. Hurry up."

I stared at him. "Eleven cups? No way."

He looked into my eyes, a look that held a new element: curiosity.

"As you have said to me in the past," he said, "we are from different worlds. Would you like to know why this is necessary?"

I considered. "I suppose so, although it won't make any difference. You can forget about the eleven cups."

He proceeded as if he hadn't heard me. "Waste, *basura toxica*, lies inside the stomach and intestines. Vomiting is an important part of your cleansing. Our people clean internally every eight or fifteen days. This keeps us from developing diseases like malaria, cholera, and yellow fever. You have toxins in your system from your sickness. They must come out."

This made some sense to me. After my diagnosis I had pored through all the literature, both mainstream and alternative, that I could find on cancer. I'd read in natural health journals that someone who has a grave illness is bogged down with unhealthy waste. The guayusa obviously worked on the same principle.

"Thanks for the explanation, Carlos. It helps me to know why I am being asked to do something that is completely foreign to me."

He looked at me with more than a touch of impatience. "There is nothing wrong with vomiting. It is *healthy* to vomit. How can you possibly think otherwise?"

Why *did* I think vomiting was disgusting or unnatural? Why did I fear it? I lifted the cup and drank.

"Another, and more quickly!" Carlos barked. I dipped and drank and dipped and drank. Nothing was coming up but my stomach felt about to explode. I was queasy but couldn't vomit; the mere idea of puking kept me from doing so.

"I can't hold any more, Carlos," I said. "I'm so filled up that I think the stuff is pouring from my eyes."

"Faster. Drink faster. *Vomit!*" he yelled.

I looked at him with hatred.

"Stick your finger down your throat."

I did it and gagged, but nothing came out of me.

"Okay," he fumed. "You will give yourself an enema with this special liquid."

"Not on your life!" It was then that I earnestly began trying to throw up so that there would be no more talk of enemas.

I drank two more cups quickly, fingering the back of my throat. Finally my body lurched. A fountain of vile liquid rocketed out. Tears squeezed from my eyes. My intestines spasmodically contracted. I became hideously dizzy, and then the worst part was upon me. I violently purged—endlessly spewed. I must have thrown up for an hour or more. Finally the cramping and pain eased and I collapsed on my hands and knees in the mud, my body exhausted and shaking.

Carlos lifted me up and took me to the piles of vomit that I had expelled. "Look here," he said. "Those small brown curly things are *bilis* (bile). The white clumps are mucus and dead cells. They are very bad to have inside you. There are many other things inside that you cannot see. Viruses and bacteria." He took me on a tour of other people's refuse, which was seeping into the forest floor. I saw small black and white worms sliding through the vomit. The worms were alive and moving!

"Those parasites came from inside someone's stomach," Carlos explained.

All of a sudden, I had to make haste and run into the bushes. It was as if my bowels were on the verge of exploding. I ripped down my pants and squatted. Piles of mushy sienna-colored stink hit the ground. I used broad leaves to clean myself. But I was stuck in the squatting position. I had not finished, not by a long shot. Enormous bugs with pincers were moving through the mulch. They looked as though they could take a big bite of my flesh. My bare behind was eaten alive by mosquitoes so small that they were almost invisible. My stomach muscles ached and my backside was raw by the time I finished.

I limped weakly back to the village, bent over and humiliated. Carlos was waiting.

"This purging seems unnatural," I whimpered. "Where I come from we don't do this kind of thing. It's so harsh!"

"Purging is very effective, physically and mentally," he answered. "In time, your spirit will grow and flower. You have made progress today."

"Maybe I did. I certainly feel cleaner." (*Roto-Rootered* is what I was thinking.) "It's so dreadful," I whined. "But something else happened during the purging."

Carlos was suddenly very interested. "Please, Margarita. Tell me what thoughts came."

"I wanted to back away like a crab from the ugly feelings that surfaced—the anger and humiliation. Fear exploded along with the vomit. My fears, my sickness, my cancer, have squeezed me so hard. After my operations I felt stagnant. So dead inside and yet so terrified of dying." I began to sob.

"*Bueno,*" said Carlos as I quieted. "I'm here to help you. Tell me exactly when this began."

"You mean the moment that fear seized me?"

"*Sí.*"

"Ten months ago I dreamed that I had cancer. A man appeared in my sleep. 'You must get help,' he said. And he indicated that the cancer was in my breast, right over my heart. The dream bothered me so much that I went to a doctor. The cancer was right where the dream man had indicated. Knowing I had the disease made me sweat with fear. It made my skin crawl. I couldn't run from the thing that was inside. All I could do was howl."

"Howl? Like a dog?" Carlos chuckled. "Just like you were howling when you were purging. It was excellent that you did that. And what else did the sickness make you do?" he asked, watching me closely.

"It sent me scurrying, first to Guatemala and now to you in Ecuador. It was as if a voice inside my head commanded me to go forth, to go out and find something. The voice ordered, *Now!* It said there was no other way. I knew I didn't want to die, but I also knew that I wanted to feel alive again, really alive, I suppose, in a way that I hadn't felt since I was a child. That is why I am here. Why I came to you."

"Margarita, this is very good news. You have done the right thing. The Great Spirit has brought you here to me. With His help and the spirit of the ayahuasca you will be healed."

"I feel greatly relieved. I believe you are going to help me."

"You are on the path of a warrior. You will go through purification, rejuvenation, and your spirit will grow strong. As a *guerrera,* you will develop courage. Margarita, you have not yet faced the many challenges awaiting you. The Red Path—the path of the warrior—is difficult and strong!"

I was surprised to be called "warrior." It implied strength and greatness and a fighting spirit. But with my raw backside and shaking knees I certainly didn't feel any of those things. The word "warrior" sounded scary, implying formidable tests to come, tests that were *dangerous!* Attila the Hun and Genghis Khan flashed through my mind's eye along with gore, terror, and spurting blood—and Mel Gibson charging into the last leg of the film *Braveheart* to die.

"In the end," Carlos continued, "the warrior understands that only he or she can battle fear. No one else can stand in his shoes. We will continue tomorrow what has begun today. At dawn, we will embark on a holy voyage."

CHAPTER THREE

Burial

Carlos would not let me eat that morning. Only three small sips of water, nothing else. I felt light and empty after my purging, as though I had been scoured from the inside out. Carlos was quiet, introspective, his motions full of deliberation and grace, almost as if he were slowly dancing to music that I couldn't hear. He made a red paste by pounding seeds in a hand-size gourd.

"Come, Margarita," he said. "We must prepare you for purification."

"Yesterday you said we were going on a holy voyage," I replied. "What did you mean?"

He didn't respond. "Sit there," he said, pointing to a log outside the kitchen area.

He turned my face upward with his hands and I felt my throat exposed. I looked at his almond eyes and slanting cheekbones, and the jungle green behind him, hot and dense in the still morning. I could hear the river running with a soft whooshing sound below me, gliding mysteriously eastward into the vast basin of the Amazon.

Carlos's eyes were blank and unfathomable, and his skin was

cool and dry. My own pores oozed in the heat, and my skin felt slick. Carlos was chanting, and he held in his hands the gourd filled with the red paste, the *achiote*.

I felt as though I wanted to weep as the warm paint touched my face. The syllables he recited were almost unbearably moving to me, and he must have felt my body tremble and the breath catch in my throat as he pushed the hair gently off my face and ran the brush made from a thin branch across my forehead and cheeks. The paint felt and smelled like wet terracotta.

He recited in a singsong tone what sounded to me like an ancient tongue, fascinating in its strangeness. My hearing skills are honed from years of writing orchestral music and listening intently to sound, but Carlos's recitation was utterly outside my frame of reference. I don't believe that I am exaggerating when I say that it sounded primordial, as though it came direct and unadulterated from a culture dating back to the Stone Age that until recently had been largely unchanged. I felt as though I were stretching my hand way back and touching the root of something at its vibrant ancient source.

I breathed it in and tried to open myself to it, but I was still so afraid. Carlos's seriousness and the hypnotic quality of his chanting helped me cope with the uneasiness that gripped me. The purging of the day before had been one of the most intense experiences of my life. Now I was about to go on a "holy voyage." What could that possibly mean? Whatever was in store, I had a strong premonition that it would be utterly new and strange and physically demanding. I was just beginning to see what an extraordinary effort I was going to have to make as Carlos continued to challenge me. I had no safe place to fall back to.

Carlos led me down to the river where Jorge, Mauro, and another young man were waiting. I didn't have a mirror, but I could imagine the way I looked, my face a mask of red designs. The men paid no attention to my appearance. Mauro's eyes darted shyly away

from mine. Even Jorge seemed subdued, as though what was tran-
spiring was beyond the carnal realm and superseded his need to
assert himself as ruler of the roost.

A dugout canoe made from a single hollowed log was beached
on the sand. Its prow was carved into a raised wooden crocodile
head with bulging eyes and a mouth full of pointed teeth.

"This is Jorge's canoe," said Carlos. "The grimacing crocodile is
his guardian."

I looked, discreetly I hoped, at Jorge's half-eaten hand. All that
was left was a pointy index finger and thumb; the last three digits
were missing. Now he seemed more complex and less a caricature
of male aggression, and this brightened my mood.

Carlos beckoned to me and I waded into the cold black water
and stepped into the canoe. I felt myself becoming excited by what
promised to be an amazing boat ride on the river. The men took
their places and Jorge paddled into the river's mighty flux. As we left
the sandbar, Jorge turned on the small outboard motor and aimed
into the white-tipped rapids at the confluence of the Puyo and
Pastaza Rivers. Jorge's bandana flapped like a flag, his shirt billowed
off his back, and his necklaces of shrunken monkey heads and
jaguar teeth were tossed around his neck. He was like a pirate at the
helm, his good hand expertly manning the rudder. The canoe
pitched and rolled, the engine churning in whorls of current. The
seams and roiling waves of the two big rivers collided. Spray hit my
face in shocks of wetness; cold drenched me. It felt heady, as if I
were on a roller coaster. I flew out of my seat and floated weightless. It was exhilarating, and I held on. I didn't have time to think,
only gape in awe. Mauro giggled.

We passed through the confluence and around a bend and the
river calmed, although it was still moving fast. There was no trace
of human presence on its banks. The jungle was virgin. Wild.
Carlos spoke: "People die on the river. Jorge has been trained over
the years in these treacherous currents."

The light and space on the open water were dazzling. The sun beat down, a fireball on my head. I hadn't thought to apply or carry my sunblock, and I knew the fair skin of my painted face and throat was sizzling. Still, the heat was delicious: I melted into it.

Jorge piloted the canoe toward a small sandy island in the middle of a wide stretch of river, an area of calm pools and broad shallow sandbars, gleaming white against the tea-colored water. When he cut the engine, the silence was empty and somehow hollow as the canoe drifted with a soft thud onto the sand.

Mauro leaped out and gripped the gunwale to steady the boat as the rest of us disembarked. I had an immediate sense of the absolute privacy of the place, its remoteness and solitude. The humidity was so high that the air seemed to rain, and my body was salty with sweat.

Speaking in Shuar, Carlos dispatched the men and then turned to me. The dread was upon me again, even before he started speaking. What could he possibly have in mind? Why had we come to this faraway place?

"Margarita," said Carlos with the utmost solemnity. "Your purification continues. It is time for you to be buried, so that you can be reborn."

Since my arrival in Ecuador, it seemed as if my life had become divided into discrete moments marked by singular and intense experiences, each like a lifetime in itself. The back streets of Quito. The jungle path. The vomiting. And now…burial?

"Is this necessary?" I asked Carlos. "Is it dangerous? Can't I be purified with holy water or prayers, something not so confrontational?"

He led me to where the men had dug a large pit in the sand. "My people have been put into the earth for centuries in preparation for that which will come. It is absolutely necessary, Margarita."

"What do I need to do? What do I need to know?"

"There is nothing for you to do. You are going to be buried in

Our Mother to prepare you for the sacred healing ritual. She will do everything that is needed. She will take all the impurities from you. Margarita, you will not be able to move, even your fingertips. Do the very best you can. I must warn you, many cannot stand to be buried under the earth and they try to thrash and escape. If you do this, it will make you think that you are going crazy or that you are going to die. Hysteria will continue until all the fight drains from you from physical exhaustion. Let the earth take you in and clean you. You will receive the power that flows from Her depths."

I was grateful that the sand looked clean, not filled with bugs and worms. Those thoughts distracted me from my nervousness. "How long are you going to make me stay here?" I asked.

He just smiled.

I stood there wondering if I could handle being covered with earth. I felt naked and alone.

"Are we ready?" Carlos asked the men, who nodded. "Margarita, get in. We will cover you now."

I took off my gum boots. I was behaving stoically, but deep down I was very, very frightened. Carlos and the crew surrounded me. I didn't know if they were there to keep me from running away or to protect me while I was in the ground.

When I was settled in the hole, the men began shoveling hot sand over me. I felt its density. The weight grew ever greater as more sand was heaped on. "You will be able to breathe through your nostrils and mouth," said Carlos. "The Mother will give you power." Then I was totally cut off from my companions and the world.

The sand cover was heavy, like lead. I lay entombed, as if I had been poured into concrete. I could breathe, but that was it. How long was I going to be left there? An hour? A day? It took all my will not to panic from claustrophobia and abandonment. I was approaching just what I had feared after my diagnosis: the trapped place of no way out and nothing left to do. I tried to shift my body, wiggle my fingers, but it was impossible. *Breathe,* I told myself. The leaves—bless them—were warm and fragrant on my face.

I became deeply aware that I hung in the balance between life and death. *You have come. You made the first step. You trusted your instincts.* I repeated this inwardly, breathing in and out and concentrating on my breath until it was even and slow and I was sinking, sliding into a dream. Although the weight was great along the surface of my skin, my thoughts floated and my mind began to wander into a soft, timeless dimension. With my ears covered, I was encased in a deep silence. I couldn't hear the blood moving through me, but I felt it thumping and pounding under my skin. I felt that the world was very far from me. Then my senses shut down.

It came to me that it was important to *surrender*, that this was the most important thing I could ever do. All my life had been about fighting, volition, deciding, choice, conflict, trying, hoping, fearing. This moment was about making that step, leaving the worried faces of my family, the downcast eyes of my friends, my doctors with their white coats and stainless steel operating tables, my world of art and music and film, and the technological wizardry that had removed us from the deep reality I was now experiencing. I was descending miles and miles into the underworld. I fell and fell. I was being demolished inside. Things that I once thought important were inconsequential. I was irrelevant, but I couldn't think about that: I had to keep astride the immense force pulling me down.

I was absorbed and my boundaries dissolved. I was in a kind of limbo, barely conscious. I could not see or feel or taste, so I listened. At first there was nothing. And then I heard something from the distance, primal sounds, sorrowful and ecstatic, from the very ground in which I lay. It came to me that what I was hearing was the roaring of the flames in the center of the earth. The earth's molten core moved toward me. I was hearing the sound of The Mother. She spoke to me in a glorious madness. Her voice was warm and entreating and all at once it seduced me. I surrendered.

There was nothing else I could do. I felt an indescribable relief more powerful than any earthly sensation I knew. I surrendered as if it were the most natural thing to do. I was mesmerized—and loved.

I "came to" vaguely terrified. I had no idea how long I'd been under. I wondered where I was. I tried to fight the intrusion of habitual consciousness, but my body would not respond. I started panicking. Something was holding me down. Where was I? Hysteria began to seethe inside me, and then I surfaced. Light struck me, hurting my eyelids. The pressure on my body began to ease.

"Leave me be," I sobbed.

Carlos and the others were exhuming me. I began to focus on their lips and eyes as their faces drew close to mine. I became aware that they were shoveling the sand away.

"No," I screamed.

I clawed the earth, trying to cover myself with it. I did not want to return to the living. I wanted to stay merged with the earth. But they lifted me by my arms and legs.

"Wake up!" Carlos commanded, and I felt little needles prickling all over my skin as my blood quickened in my veins. The men hoisted me into a standing position, but my legs buckled. My muscles would not work.

"I must go back," I wept. "Don't make me leave. Keep away from me."

Carlos took me from the men and held me under my arm, putting his other arm around my waist. Almost carrying me, he forced me away from the burial site. "We must leave this place now," he said very gently, his breath in my ear. Still I fought him, thrashing, but my arms did not have much power in them.

"Come, Margarita," he said, almost chanting. "This is not a place we can stay. The umbilical is cut. But we are still connected. You will see."

"I don't want to leave," I panted, my head hanging on my chest, my eyes closed, my wrists limp, my ankles wobbly.

"Do not worry," he said. "Everything is fine. Everything is as it should be. Come with me now, Margarita. Let me lead you into the warm waters. Let me lead you into the shallow pools of the Pastaza. Our people have used this sacred place for just this purpose for as long as we can remember. You will float in birthing fluids. You have been purified, reborn from the womb of The Mother."

The sun was low in the sky, hanging over the unruly ramparts of the jungle that tumbled down to the river. The black stain of the water was lit with a golden sheen. Carlos helped me lie down in the tepid shallows. As soon as I entered the water, everything shifted, and I no longer struggled or mourned. I blissfully drifted, feeling as if I was a newborn and had just entered the world. I really was purified—a great emotional weight had lifted. It was as if a light was shining out from my chest and stomach and I had a profound feeling of well-being. I felt more solid than before. No, more *physical*.

I could see the sun sending out tongues of flame thousands of miles into space. I could feel the force beyond all reckoning that made its fire cohere, take shape, and I felt the tangible connection between the warmth it was sending out and the life all around and inside me.

It seemed pointless to remember that I had come to the Amazon because of a grave illness. At that moment, I couldn't evaluate what I had experienced. Before Ecuador, I would have considered the burial and vomiting insane tests of endurance. Now they seemed simply to be what you went through because you were human and alive.

As I drifted, my analytic mind began to work again, but it was still far away, a distant voice. I dimly grasped that my ego had dissolved during the burial. I understood how that experience could be both liberating and dangerous—ah, that way madness lies. And yet I knew that it was impossible to grow without being broken.

What I didn't know was that Carlos was preparing me for even greater ecstatic and perceptual shifts that would come.

"You are now ready to take the sacred medicine, Margarita," Carlos said as he helped me out of the shallows and walked me back to the canoe. Fear, like a stake, drove into my heart—even with my newfound equanimity and the feeling that I had just passed through fire and endured.

It was a terrifying prospect—ayahuasca. I wanted to keel over. Then I noticed Jorge was leering at me again. There was nothing furtive or abashed in the way he studied my body. In fact, there was something admirable in his complete lack of pretence. Keeping his eyes glued to my breasts, he leaned back, dug his paddle in the sand, and pried. The canoe broke free from the island where I had been reborn and glided out into the dark water. Jorge leaned forward and I could see the ropy muscles pop in his forearm as he ripped the cord of the outboard and the engine snarled and died and he ripped the cord again. The engine sputtered, raced, and then settled into a dull whine. Jorge turned the canoe in a long arc and pointed the crocodile head with its gaping mouth upriver. He cranked the throttle, and I felt the prow rise, pushing against the current. I was shivering, despite the heat.

Carlos gazed at me steadily. "You must not back down, Margarita," he said. "Be fearless. This is your path. This is what it means to be *kakaram*, a warrior of valor."

CHAPTER FOUR

Vine of the Maestros

The men were silent on the canoe ride back to Jorge's compound. I gazed at herons perched on logs and saw the exposed roots of great trees rising from the water's edge. When we reached the settlement it got dark instantly. I went immediately to my sleeping area. Carlos let me be. I had no desire to speak with anyone and didn't go down for dinner that night. When I was hungry, I ate two energy bars. I suppose the day's events were working on me, partially in an unconscious manner. Thoughts formed:

Our bodies speak to us, but we must listen. Our bodies are vehicles to access intuition. This was my first insight into the ability to know something immediately without the need for conscious reasoning.

My body has been sending me signals for quite some time. It even sent me the dream telling me to see a doctor. I couldn't reason this out. I felt the truth in this dream, but not in a logical manner. Intuition revealed its presence to me at first as dream symbols; then it became a feeling, and then an idea that required action. The dream's core value had nothing to do with a logical, concrete thinking process.

Intuition is a *knowing* that precedes conscious thought. Maybe, I thought, intuition is another word for honesty—knowing what *is*, rather than acting on wishes, hopes, or denial. Our body is a reservoir of information, and it is ruthlessly honest. Intuition is something we can know with certainty and act on with conviction. In retrospect, I see what Carlos was beginning to teach me was that wanting to be honest was the first step a warrior had to take.

The quiet voice in my head said, *You are attempting to remove the clutter and inner static that has accumulated.* I knew at that moment that I was going to listen to and deepen my relation to my intuition. The voice continued: *It is all happening because you need it to happen and because it is time.*

I looked around the sleeping room. It smelled woody because of the dampness, but a night breeze blew through the open windows. Sleepy, I lay down on my cot, but I did not hear anyone else from the group crawl into bed that night.

Early the next morning, Carlos and I drank herbal tea Tia had prepared for us. We quickly ate a few plantains and then Carlos grabbed his machete. I lathered myself in sunscreen. We walked away from Jorge's compound in the direction of the crocs' lagoons. We were going to harvest ayahuasca.

We waded through shallow black-water streams that drained into a swamp. At one point, I was drawn to look at my reflection in one of the stagnant ponds. I looked vaguely familiar, but somehow I was not the "me" who had come to Ecuador. My hair was sticking out, and my face looked tiny, blackened, with crossing lines…or perhaps those were only small eddies or twigs in the water.

Traveling mostly on well-worn paths, we came to an area alongside one of the larger streams. Carlos had to hack the dense brush with a machete to carve a way through. We moved into the foliage and away from the riverbank. Insects shrilled, birds cawed, swamp frogs croaked. Gnarled vines, thick as a man's thigh, or thin and curly like string, hung down from the forest canopy, lianas criss-crossing in chaos. I thought I was hearing things with more acuity. I somehow felt that I should listen patiently. My awareness became unusually attentive to the sound of my own footfalls and to the hums and buzzes that surrounded us. We were a half hour's distance by foot from Jorge's.

"I have a strong connection with *la medicina* here," said Carlos. He seemed to greet the ayahuasca as if he were coming to pay respects to a relative.

The vines in this special area were long, ropey, and coiled. Some were about the diameter of a wrist, but others were as thin as pencils. Carlos meticulously selected the ones he wanted. It appeared he chose them for size and strength and other attributes invisible to my eyes. When he cut the vines, they were strips ten feet or more in length, entangled in foliage and wrapped around one another. He had to bring each one out carefully. The cutting and untangling took time and patience, and he insisted on getting the precise vine he wanted each time. I helped him unwind the lianas and hold them outstretched as he cut them.

"Collecting the best vines is an exacting art," he said. "One must speak with the plant. The lianas each have their various potencies. These will yield the greatest vision."

After he selected and extracted specific vines, Carlos cut the lengths into three-foot sections with his machete. He knelt to pick up one of the larger chunks and gazed into its cross-section. Its pith was heart-shaped, and he said it contained the wisdom and core knowledge of the jungle. It was the heart of the Mother.

Carlos pointed out the layered sections to me. "The bark is used around garden plants because the insects hate it and leave the vegetables growing peacefully," he told me. "The choice of the vine and the way the liana is harvested and stored play an important part in preparing for an ayahuasca ritual. There are many invisible influences surrounding the preparation of the medicine."

Carlos bundled the lianas with stringlike vines for transport. He said prayers and sang to them. Then we took cuttings from the largest pieces. "We must plant two shoots from these vines we have cut from the mother plants," he said. "We will plant a male and a female so that they may be available for our future relatives. These vines I have chosen for our ritual tonight were planted by *ancianos* more than fifty years ago. They are very powerful. There are at least one hundred and twenty varieties of ayahuasca. The cuttings that are planted by the *maestros* not only keep the lineage alive, but because they are the strongest and most powerful types, they are most prized by uwishins. You will watch me make the medicine, and tonight we will drink from the vines of my predecessors, my teachers."

There were four main structures in the center of Jorge's compound. My sleeping place was next to Tia's kitchen and across from a long open structure called the ceremonial longhouse. The fourth structure was a lean-to, which functioned as a secondary kitchen for cooking medicine. Like the other buildings, it was made from bamboo lashed together and sunk into the earth.

When Carlos and I returned to camp, we entered the lean-to hut. The high ceiling was made of thatched palm-leaf bundles. In the dimness, long shafts of light striped the beaten earth floor. Under the fringed line of the palm roofing, the forest vegetation outside was dazzling. We were alone. The men were off in the forest tending their corn and tobacco crops. Tia was nowhere in sight, and the young women and children had also disappeared. I would later learn that they did not want to be close to the ayahuasca when it was cooking, because of its power.

The firewood had already been gathered, by whom I did not know, and I was waiting for Carlos to ceremoniously light the wooden logs. When the flames were hot enough, he placed a large black kettle with about four gallons of water on the fire. While we waited for the water to boil, Carlos and I pounded the three-foot segments of vine with a log until the pulp was feathery and splintered. This took over an hour. Then Carlos placed the carefully prepared plant fibers in the kettle.

I stood by as Carlos stirred the vines of the maestros in the water. He occasionally explained what he was doing, but mostly he wanted no interruptions. I sensed that the practice of making the potion was a secluded endeavor, not so much a secret (although it may have been that) but a process that should be free from disturbing or disruptive influences. It was complex, the ritual and prayers precise, and Carlos was deeply engrossed in the actions and intention it required. He wasn't in a trance, but he was tightly focused.

Carlos added fresh green leaves and the scraped bark of other plants to the brew, praying all the while. He organized everything with meticulous care and great reverence, fussing over the caldron lovingly. "Ayahuasca's true potency depends on its spiritual nature," he said. "This must be considered in the preparation, and in the intent of the ceremony in which it will be utilized."

The smell of the ayahuasca as it cooked was feral and slightly nauseating, mixing with the primordial smells from the fire and the odors of the rotting forest. And my own preparation was taking place within me. As I stood there watching Carlos work, I felt the utmost respect—and fear.

The ayahuasca bubbled wildly over the fire, reminding me of a witch's cauldron. Carlos tended it constantly. If it boiled over or burned, it would be a grave disaster. The ayahuasca would punish anyone who requested visions after being so careless. Even Carlos was fearful of the terror that would rain down on him if he were to violate the plant.

It was late afternoon, still, hot, and humid. The medicine fire burned and the ayahuasca cooked. I asked Carlos if I could have a tiny sip of water, knowing that the next time I could drink would be the following morning. He nodded.

When the mixture was thick and dark, Carlos filtered the vegetable sediments out through a strainer. As soon as the ayahuasca cooled down, the decoction would be ready for consumption.

Carlos explained what would happen to me during the upcoming ceremony.

"You have been forbidden certain foods because you must fast before rituals with the sacred medicine. This morning you were allowed a few boiled plantains and water. Until tomorrow your intake of water must be minimal. Your stomach must be empty when you drink ayahuasca.

"After you drink the medicine tonight your body will get very cold. This will most likely begin at your feet and take up to one half hour. But it is necessary that you *let* it happen. Wear as little clothing as possible. Your body should be cold to battle sickness and the dark forces. Once the medicine is in your body, the spirit will depart from your flesh. You may journey to the unseen worlds or receive visions."

Carlos showed me the other plants that had gone into the medicine: leaves of plants he called *yagé*, a green shiny leaf about one inch long, which is also known as *chacruna* (*Psychotria viridis*). There was also *semirok*, the Shuar name for a reddish brown–colored bark. I still don't know what plant this is; semirok could be a special ingredient Carlos used for his personal concoctions.

"Each plant contains a spirit, an invisible being," Carlos said. "They hold great wisdom and power, and they can heal. My people call ayahuasca *natem*. For millennia we have used this medicine to part the veils covering our spiritual eyes."

CHAPTER FIVE

The Holy Terror

A round nine, Carlos led the locals and me into the dim light of a communal longhouse. A sympathetic woman directed us to take our places in the ceremonial space. In the open area stood a tall middle-aged Andean man named Jaime who had traveled with us from Quito. Also present were Carlos's son Mauro and various members of the community. Relatives of Tia and Jorge appeared. Others arrived whom I had never seen before. I realized that there could be other villages around Jorge's compound, hidden by the hilly terrain and thick growth. Jorge and Tia were nowhere to be seen.

I took a seat on a log. I was anxious about the medicine, what I had named "the holy terror" after my initiation in Guatemala. But Carlos had convinced me that drinking it was nonnegotiable. "You are choosing your path, your destiny to live."

Tonight Carlos had carefully decorated his face, tracing lines of red geometric patterns on his skin. He wore seed anklets and a simple headdress, a corona of red and yellow toucan feathers. An ornament made of bird bones was wrapped around his shoulders like a bandolier, signifying the possession of an *arutam* soul—a kind of power obtained by one who has battled apparitions such as gigantic jaguars or anacondas. Wresting power from such formidable spirits becomes manifest in a man's persona by means of his strong voice, his authority within his society, and his behavior in the face of danger.

Carlos greeted each of us formally; then he took his place behind the altar to rearrange his ritual paraphernalia: his bottles of liquid medicines, *aguardiente,* 150-proof cane alcohol for cleansing the spirit of a patient, quartz crystals, and a fan of leaves. Jaime played a palpating rhythm on a barrel-shaped hand drum. It sounded solemn, like a dirge.

"Tonight I desire that all of the cosmic and earthly forces vibrate with strength in our bodies," Carlos said. "We are prepared. We are ready and purified. I have much faith that the sacred medicine will take hold in our bodies and will open the portal dimensions so that we can visualize the Great Spirit."

He lifted one of the bottles filled with ayahuasca and began to sing in Shuar, invoking the spirits and asking that those in need be healed. He sang to the spirits of the land and the water, the cosmos and the stars, and to the Tsunquis, hermaphroditic spirits of the waters, whom he asked to visit us that night. He prayed solemnly for those who were hungry, sick, alone, or in pain. For twenty minutes, he sang over the ayahuasca and breathed into it, making a forceful whooshing sound as he drove his breath into the mixture.

"I pray that the Mother Earth is together with us and that the spirits—the greatest maestros and those of knowledge who have passed from this planet—are together with us, to give us light, to give us life, to give us power, and to give us the way of truth. I pray that with our spiritual eyes we may look upon these superior forces."

Pouring *la medicina* from plastic Coke bottles, Carlos offered it to each person in a small hard seedpod cup. He moved among us, solemn and serene, handling the cup with precision and studied inflection. He endowed the proceedings with a theatrical flare, commanding the moment, delineating the space. Jaime dutifully took his place in front of Carlos and accepted his portion of the ayahuasca, grimacing as he drank the potion. Carlos snapped at Jaime for acting childishly. Others took their turns.

"Drink it quickly," said Carlos. Doubtful, tormented, I raised it to my lips. The liquid was as dark and viscous as molasses. Carlos's stare was searing; he nodded, motioning for me to drink. I swallowed the cup in one gulp. The taste was acrid and putrid at once, like the entire jungle rotting on my tongue. My mouth and throat revolted against it. But I sat quietly among the Shuar and the Quechua, conscious of the power and authority of the ritual, as Carlos drank his potion.

Then Carlos stood up and began chanting as he played his violin. The rest of us waited. The only light came from the fire burning in the center of the room. The floor was pounded dirt, the overhead palm thatch, the sides of the longhouse open to the elements. The fire grew bigger and roared. Carlos's voice grew bolder. The violin, at times delicate and at other times strident, skimmed the shell of my eardrums. There followed Carlos's high, tremulous voice and the sound of rattles and anklets. A half hour or more passed. Mauro, who was sitting next to me, gently swayed and moaned. Looking around, I noticed the villagers sprawled on the packed earth floor, inert against one another. Mauro was now holding his head in his hands; I watched as he slumped down on all fours. I reached out to him with loving maternal feelings and his back trembled beneath my hand. He curled into the fetal position. I slid down to help him but could not wake him. Carlos's annoyance flashed in his eyes. He'd been expecting Mauro to help him in the night's work, but Mauro was incapacitated. Jaime retched, crawled outside the hut, and disappeared. A villager stood and vomited down the front of his ripped T-shirt. Others slumped, heads hanging limply.

I could hear everything with unaccustomed clarity; the roaring river, the constant hum of the insects, and the croaking frogs droned in my ears with equal intensity. I waited for what seemed like an endless period for the medicine to take hold. Maybe it would not be as bad as I expected. Maybe the medicine wouldn't work on me, and I could get up and go to bed!

But suddenly the violin soared and the musical line flew into the air. It screeched like a locomotive. The music moved through ever-widening spirals and parabolic curves. Time was expanding and receding as the music pulled on me. It seemed as if my pupils had dilated in order to see more. The cells in my ears could hear a twig crack hundreds of yards away. The air took on a magnetic quality, splitting into particles.

A cold tingling rose from my feet through my core. I was terrified. *Is this how the body feels as the soul departs?* Wind vaulted through the trees. Sight and sound got mixed up. Stars pushed across the sky like a De Kooning abstract canvas—but they roared! The floodgates in my brain were wide open and images and sounds rushed through. It was the dream state, experience changing and morphing, leaping back and forth through decades, centuries. Through the looking glass.

As I struggled to get my bearings, I spied a point of reference: a gnomish man, with dark beady eyes and mustache, cavorting before me. Somehow I understood that he was the gatekeeper. "Come here," he said. "I want to show you *las plantes sagradas*." He opened the snaky leaves of a lush tropical plant, inviting me for a look into the livid hues of green. Thin dark stripes drew me down into the plant's core, leading me through its veins and cells. The man was ten feet from me, but I could see his hands as clearly as if I were putting my face into his palms.

Through its lips, the plant began to describe its powers. "You are welcome," it said. "Come in. My power to see inside things, I bestow on you. My power to see from multiple vantage points, I give to you. Look up."

The stars zoomed down from the heavens, turning into electric particles in the air around me, inside me. I was in the spaces between them. I looked skyward and saw Carlos flying to the four corners above the group. I was in the sky, following him, and I understood that he was cordoning off the area for our protection.

Boom! Carlos was earthbound, moving among us, spraying a liquid from his mouth. It was aguardiente, jungle juice that he had infused with *agua de florida* and herbs. Its icy mist seared my face and shoulders. Some people screamed when he blasted them with it. I began to shake violently. Penetrating shadows paced. A black jaguar stalked through the night.

My sinuses vibrated and my skull shimmied. The jaguar circled the area. A growl rose from my throat as an aggressive female jaguar came into my body. My hands turned into paws, claws extended.

Carlos and I growled and sparred, articulating a domain. He tried to dominate me. I fought for territorial rights—for the right to *survive*. Others who had been limp now peered at us, petrified. Splayed frequencies ripped away my mind, tore into the fabric of the universe. I felt that I was on the razor's edge where life meets death. It was thrilling and terribly real, the edge of the unknown.

Carlos's fan of condor feathers smacked me on the head. He instructed me to go sit in front of him. Once I was seated, his chanting turned into a soft whistling sound that blew over me. While he sang, he swept my body with the *shiri-shiri*, the sheath of leaves used by the shaman to cleanse and to call the helper spirits. The jaguar abruptly left my body.

Carlos looked into me, through me, and began to pull some-thing from my chest, right where my cancer was. I could feel the sickness being sucked out. He worked quickly and methodically, drawing a black smoke from my flesh, shooting it out into space where its particles vanished. When he shook a rattle over me, a cold silver aura enveloped my body. He drove a forceful breath into the top of my skull. It rushed through me with a powerful surge—a quiver of tiny arrows that struck through to my groin. He hit me again with the aguardiente, and I shrieked.

As he passed the fan over me again, he snapped his wrists as if to discharge the energy. I heard him whisper in my ear, "Look inside where you are hurt."

Every cell in my body twinkled like starlight. The cells were alive and pulsing. They were beating the rhythm of the cosmos. Some were spontaneously regenerating, sending live signals to others beside them. The dark spots in my breast were black holes sucking energy into another sphere, one in which living things were doomed.

Carlos was pressing hard and swirling his fingertips deep into fleshy parts of me where the black smoke lay. I cried in pain. His touch was intimate and at the same time not so. The force he used was harsh and also practical. Many times his touch was physically painful as he tugged dark smoky ribbons from me, black ribbons of sickness. I watched as Carlos's hand magnetized the black smoke. It spread like army ants in file and followed his motion away from my body.

Carlos was sucking on me again. Then he pulled away to spit a foul substance onto the ground. He growled as if he had something caught in his throat. He spat again, barked like a jaguar, and then he whistled a long sound blast skyward.

I wanted to squeeze myself back into my former unknowingness, but that was impossible. A feeling of deep sadness came over me. I felt as if I were exposed in all my frailty and weakness.

Carlos sang over me and breathed into the crown of my head, sending a feeling of well-being through me, the sense that a curative energy was filling my body. I felt transparent but also concrete and powerful. Never before had I experienced anything so vivid and alive. My body befitted me, more so than I had known or appreciated. I was aware of the fullness of who I was, and it was an ecstatic feeling.

Ecstasy was a potent medicine, I thought. The power that

passed through Carlos into me, what was it? Union with creation? I hummed with an immense, joyous vitality. As dawn was breaking, I found myself at peace, but I knew my life had been profoundly changed.

Before coming to Ecuador, it had seemed that even the *potential* for joy had been driven from me, never to return. I sat in the ceremonial longhouse reviewing the horrors I'd survived just to get to the point of feeling peace. Carlos believed that his medicines could purify the body and release the subconscious contents that can cause illness. Was this what had happened to me?

Yes. I had released toxins from my body, and the emotional part of me *had* started flowing. Something seemed to have shifted on a cellular level. I believed Carlos had touched the roots of my disease, which I began to suspect were fear, repression, the calcification of love and the life force within me. I didn't know what was coming next, but at that moment, I decided that there was no turning back from it.

CHAPTER SIX

The Jungle Lives in Us

The next morning, after a few hours' sleep, Carlos woke me and told me to follow him. He led me down a path snaking away from Jorge's compound. We passed a mud puddle where hundreds of small yellow butterflies hovered. Their weightless wings and vivid color vibrated deliciously through me. The evening before seemed like an ancient dream, and I felt possessed by its mystery.

When we reached a flat rock overhanging a tributary of the Puyo River, Carlos motioned to sit down and then he sat beside me.

The equatorial sun and fat clouds were immobile in the sky. The sun warmed the rock's surface. Peering down into the clear water, I followed the stream cascading down a steep slope, racing toward the raging river that I had traveled in the crocodile canoe. The bottom of the stream was strewn with stones. The Pastaza, a large tributary to the Amazon River sounded in the distance, loud, then barely audible, modulating with hypnotic irregularity.

"Carlos," I said, "the visions I saw last night were so incomprehensible, impossible for me to understand. Yet they were also vivid and real, more so than being here with you now. I felt as if I were flying at one point…and then I was, well, possessed by that jaguar."

"Ah, yes, you were indeed!" He laughed, grabbed hold of my hair, and flipped it in the air. "She arrived in the swells of hurricane winds and swooped violently into you. You fought to survive. You clawed and growled. She gave you strength—and tested you."

"I sure as hell did fight. But what *really* happened?" I patted my hair back into place.

"My spirit is that of the black jaguar," Carlos explained. He would later tell me that the jaguar is a shape-shifter—one of the most powerful spirit helpers an uwishin can have—and the rare black ones have particular power.

"Yes, I saw that! How could we both experience the same thing?"

"With the assistance of the sacred medicine you were able to see. Visions do not come readily until the body has been cleansed, and for some they do not come. But natem is teaching you."

"I felt as if I was getting direct knowledge. I want to understand—but I can't take this in!"

"Margarita, natem is a living presence, a spirit and a guide."

"Can you describe what you mean by spirit?"

"A spirit can be animal, insect, human, stone, plant, or star. Spirits are animated beings with intelligence. Each type has different kinds and degrees of power. They are most easily seen in complete darkness."

"Why did it all seem so real?"

"The dimensional worlds, the dream world, and the world we touch with our physical hands are all real. Everything in the universe is real and natural. Every human being has spiritual eyes that can see and feel spirits, plants, and animals, which themselves can see or speak with us. Each one of us has five physical senses and five spiritual senses. Normally, man never uses the five spiritual senses and for that reason he cannot 'see.' Margarita, you are being given the opportunity to open your nonphysical senses."

So the jaguar wasn't a figment of my imagination—or were Carlos and I intertwined in a folie à deux? But others at the ceremony had seen us fighting as jaguars too! I had thought that knowledge gained through direct contact with my eyes, ears, nose, mouth, and hands was my only means of sensory perception, but as Carlos spoke I began to consider that natem might have helped me *perceive* using other, nonphysical senses. This possibility threw me into agonizing disarray.

Carlos stood up, letting me know that the conversation was over, and he stripped down to his underwear. I watched in mild shock, wondering what was about to happen. Frankly, I was surprised that he even owned underwear. He dove into the river, swam around, and reached down between the rocks. Then he stood up dripping water, his face gleaming, his wide smile boyish and proud. His unadulterated enjoyment resonated with the beauty of the water, sky, and trees. But my mind was racing. Was Carlos priming me for something other than my own healing? Why was all this knowledge coming to me?

Carlos was grasping a wriggling something in his bare hands. Before I knew it, a slimy thing flew through the air and landed, flapping, on my lap. I jumped up. "Carlos, don't you throw anything else from the water at me!"

"Hold it. I'm getting more for our breakfast."

I looked at the suckerfish. Its mouth pulsed open and closed, drawing with a powerful force to breathe. It was gray, small, slippery, without scales; it looked like a trilobite.

Carlos hurled another fish at me. Then he pulled a vine from the riverbank, wrapped the long string around his waist, and swaggered about outrageously. He was a trickster and a clown as he crossed the river on his sturdy legs to splash me. I yelled at him but he paid no attention and lunged out of the water, grabbing my leg and trying to pull me, fully clothed, into the river.

I escaped his grasp and dived behind the roots of a giant tree.

He came at me again, dripping wet and close to naked. I wasn't really scared, but I had no idea how to deal with his juvenile and slightly menacing behavior. I decided that the best strategy was not to play along. He taunted; I feigned boredom. He made funny faces; I barely cracked a smile. I was relieved when he lost interest and earnestly began hunting for breakfast. It was a pleasure to watch him move about in the river, diving, grabbing and then stringing the fish. They thrashed against his body.

He came up out of the river, his body muscular and fit, and handed me the string of wiggling fish. Why do men always hand women things to hold for them? I wondered. Couldn't he just put them on the rock? He slid back into his pants; slicked back his long hair, and we went to Tia's for breakfast.

Carlos prayed, as he always did before eating. I gave thanks to be back in the world as I knew it—a world not populated by bizarre and menacing creatures. We breakfasted on boiled, boney trilobites and plantain. I was beginning to see that in the village food was never relished for its taste—it was sustenance, typical fare. But when meat was available, or when food was brought back from Puyo, Tia prepared chicken and cooked vegetables wrapped in banana leaves cooked over an open fire.

I walked back to the secluded spot that Carlos and I had shared earlier that morning to bathe in the river. I looked around carefully before taking off my clothes, then gingerly entered the river. It was freezing cold and filled with God knows what. I would have loved to immerse myself in a steamy porcelain bathtub with fragrant salts and then put on new, dry clothes. But the intermittent rain kept everything I had constantly damp and my clothes clung to me like slime. I dunked quickly, soaped up, and then clambered back up the bank.

The morning heat, already intense, felt delicious after the icy water. I breathed in deeply. I thought about the ceremony and the aliveness it had given me. I thought about my privations here in the

jungle, which were many. But the physical trials and the lack of
what I'd considered necessities were made up for by this new sense
of adventure and awe.

Days ran together. Carlos and I explored the jungle around
Jorge's small village. He believed that the natural world was a reservoir of profound wisdom and he wanted me to see how the natural
world existed within the physical body. "I want to pass this knowledge on to you," he said. "It's part of your healing."

Jorge, Carlos, Mauro, and I visited other villages. We engaged
in terrible climbing treks, and I was constantly slipping and
sliding and stumbling over great roots and gnarled tendrils. The
men teased me mercilessly when I ripped open the seat of my
pants *and* my underpants on a jagged branch while climbing up a
cliff of mud and twisted roots. They traveled right under my bare
bottom as we climbed upward for a good hour. At other times,
they dangled me over a cliff, showed me in dead earnest a path
back down to our village by way of a ninety-degree drop, and then
laughed themselves silly when I believed they were seriously
considering the route.

In other villages, Carlos and I played soccer in the rain with
distant relatives, collected rocks at the river, and found *huacas*,
sacred healing stones that had come with volcanic lava washed
down with mountain snows. I saw short-limbed, fleshy-snouted
tapirs, and I held what must have been the world's smallest monkey,
not much bigger than a hamster, in my shirt pocket.

We'd return in the late afternoons to Jorge's compound, where
Carlos played the fiddle, accompanied by Mauro on the flute and
Jorge on a wooden drum that he had carved in the shape of a crocodile. I recorded Carlos singing ritual songs and chatted with the
parrots in front of Tia's kitchen. At night, there were often ceremonies with natem, and I continued my explorations into the
dimension of spirits.

Time flowed and I got used to walking through the forest with Carlos. In spite of the sheer physical effort of scaling the wild terrain, these stark encounters with pristine nature left me in a state of purity and harmony. I had attended a Baptist church when I was young, but there was no relation between those empty rituals and the reverence I felt communing in the church of Nature. As the jungle drew me closer to God and Creation, I found my way back to grace. I saw the interconnectedness and interdependence of the natural world and I understood that humans were not superior, just a part of the great cosmos.

The rain forest's magnificence was matched by its violence: Vines and tendrils strangled one another to reach the sun. The smell of decomposition was everywhere. Thunderstorms boomed over the land, and there was constant danger from crocs, snakes, quicksand, malaria, yellow fever, cholera, and so on. In the jungle life was brighter, death quicker. The hunter and the hunted intertwined.

We climbed sheer mud cliffs or descended into treacherous valleys. The terrain was almost never flat. I had to reach out to vines and roots to pull myself up, and when I slipped, I'd grab hold of anything I could. Carlos would haul me up, righting me.

He showed me snakes looped like bracelets in the trees. "Never use your hands to climb," he explained. "There are snakes that wrap themselves around the branches and vines. They are everywhere. You must keep your hands close to your body. Watch where you step—every moment! We have poisonous snakes. One is so deadly that if you're bitten, in a very short time you'll start bleeding, hemorrhaging from the eyes, nose, ears, and mouth. You'll be dead in a few hours. We have plants to treat these bites, but they are not always successful."

The snake Carlos spoke about and pointed out to me, half hidden in rotting leaves, was small, brown, and nondescript and looked as harmless as a garden snake. It was a *Bothrops*! I would later read in a herpetology book that the venom of this species of viper, called fer-de-lance in the vernacular, is painful, hemotoxic, and hemorrhagic. It causes massive tissue destruction that makes the cell walls rupture. The body gushes blood as the organs turn to mush.

As Carlos and I moved through the jungle, the heat, the humid mists, and the whooshing of his machete began to work on me. I sweated, inhaled the moist air, and gathered strength. Carlos gripped the machete, with its eighteen-inch-long blade of stainless steel, loosely between his thumb and forefinger, and then curved the blade up in an arc as he hacked at bushes and vines. The swinging metal mesmerized me with its constant ringing. Random but effective, his motion broke through newly grown foliage that covered narrow animal trails.

One day we came to a stand of bamboo. Carlos harvested a dozen or so stalks for making flutes. Then he slashed deftly through a tall tree with a slim trunk; smooth, mottled bark; and large, heart-shaped bright green leaves. A thick ooze of resin dripped from the wound in the trunk. He called it the "blood tree."

"I know hundreds of medicines that come from the plants and animals that I use on my patients," he said. "*Mira.* See the blood flow from this tree? We use *sangre de drago,* dragon's blood, on open sores. The sap can stop wounds from bleeding. It is also used externally for fractures and hemorrhoids and internally for intestinal blockages, stomach ulcers, and uterine problems.

"The jungle has plants that will cure anything. Do you suppose the Great Spirit would send disease that did not also have an antidote?"

Carlos pointed out the lipstick tree, *Bixa orellana*, whose dark, spiky seedpod, the size of a golf ball, contained the achiote seeds used for painting facial designs. He showed me small pale seeds of various hues and shapes, along with a flattish walnut-colored seed called the Eye of the Deer, which was used to make ritual necklaces, although they were poisonous to eat. Seeds and fruits in all stages of decay lay on the ground. The smells, sweet and sometimes putrid, gave a sharp edge to the idyll. Occasionally, I could smell the rot of a carcass somewhere close by.

Ferns that looked like fiddleheads, but with hairy platter-size curvatures on four-foot stalks, lazed in the wet heat. Drenched leaves the size of elephant ears brushed against my shoulders and chest. The jungle was anything but quiet. The constant music of buzzing and humming insects would suddenly be broken with the shrieking blast of toucans and macaws rocketing through the canopy. Monkeys flew overhead. The dense air smoldered. Sometimes mist hung in the air, and the rains came with a smashing thunder that was so loud it drowned out all other sound.

The seemingly countless plants, I learned from Carlos, were mostly poisonous. Their alkaloids kept insects from consuming them, and those same chemicals were deadly to humans and animals when ingested. Carlos told me that vegetables such as beans, squash, and tomatoes could not be cultivated in the jungle because the insects devoured them before harvest. Yucca, plantains, tobacco, and ayahuasca could be cultivated, as well as cocoa and some fruit trees.

I sensed Carlos wanted me to learn and retain what he was telling me. But so many of the plants looked alike, I could never cross-reference them because Carlos didn't know the Spanish or Latin names, and since I'm not a botanist, most of this information was lost to me. There was ayahuasca; wild guayusa; *floripondio*, a notoriously potent "plant of power" that could leave a person in an altered state for three days; *una de gato*, an herbal preparation made from bark, stems, and leaves and used as an immune system builder; *wampum*, a Shuar name for a sap used for amoebas and diarrhea; *cedrón*, from the mint family, used as a tea for its tranquilizing effect; *ruda*, used in the aguardiente and helpful for blood and nervous problems; a tree whose green leaves were used as an infusion to treat diabetes; *uva*, a shrub whose fruit helped with influenza; *coca*, which Carlos told me was milder than the mountain type; as well as mints, chamomile, vanilla pods, medicines for liver ailments, fevers, heart problems, and more. There were several types of palm, mahogany, and cedar.

Carlos showed me the vine sacks that women wove into baskets for carrying large quantities of vegetables and other materials, as well as the vines, trees, nut shells, and clay that were used to make furniture, bowls, utensils, and clothes. Palm thorns became arrows. Palm trunks were used for timbers, planks, fiber; palm fronds for fences and thatching, functional for building homes.

"Margarita, I can build a bamboo and palm house in a day," Carlos said. "I am self-sufficient in the jungle. I can make bows and arrows, curare, build a fire, and make more than two hundred medicines, gather fruit, make clothes, hunt, and fish. With my machete, I am complete. Survival in *la selva,* though, is very, very difficult.

"When the Spanish came five hundred years ago, they told the Shuar that we were uncivilized savages who lived in the jungle like animals. But this is not true. My people told the *conquistadores*: 'We do not live in the jungle. The jungle lives in us.'

"Margarita, I am at one with her. I am not *in* the jungle. The jungle is within me. The wisdom I hold cannot be learned from a book, but from the earth, which sends its voice through my body. We are one and the same."

CHAPTER SEVEN

Spirit of the Waters

During these weeks, as Carlos and I explored the jungle by day, the fasting, purging, and visions continued in the nighttime healing ceremonies. We drank *la medicina sagrada* an average of three nights a week. Though I was feeling much better, I'd wondered about my own healing. But Carlos had told me not to ask him how I was doing, just to be intimately involved in everything that I was experiencing. And then, without realizing it, I'd simply become engrossed. "I am" became completely lost in actions and freedom from self-consciousness. Being in the jungle with Carlos was mesmerizing. Ecstasy in all its forms abounded, as did experiences of horror and pain. Still, there was more to come.

The ayahuasca brought up the fear, the ugliness, and the dead parts inside of me. Visions of otherworldly creatures and surreal places could appear ecstatic and horrifying at the same moment. Menacing spirits could appear to terrify me. I saw snakes; the open jaws of an anaconda as wide as a garage door; screaming, melting "things." These, I was told, could actually hurt me—Carlos said this was possible if he were not there to protect me—but they had come to force me to gather courage and fight.

Sometimes the visions were almost comically bizarre. One night, the natem spirit threw washing machines and televisions at me. Microwave ovens flew past jungle palms and mahogany trees. Insects gathered, whispering among themselves, pointing at me. Masked creatures leered. I cringed and begged for mercy.

"Hah!" said a disembodied voice, or was it the washing machine? "Your quaint, cozy home. The appurtenances of your oh-so-comfortable life. You stand at the very abyss of death and nothingness."

Appliances continued to assault me. "Become your own hero. Sink or swim. Sink or swim," the phantasms said.

"Live with conviction and stand strong like a warrior," Carlos reminded me. "This is a humbling process, but as you have chosen the Red Path, every action must be carried out responsibly and with love."

Carlos showed me how to sit in such a way that the angles of my body were open, and to hold that pose for hours. He explained that the posture most people sit in cuts off their energy at the pubic bone. I learned to sit straight with my body awake as visions rushed through my head at dizzying speed. Carlos called this "staying sober" on the medicine. I could walk around, get instructions from the medicine visions, and be aware of my surroundings. I could control my reactions to the visions and stay grounded.

Ayahuasca seemed to be trying to make me into a better and more compassionate human being. I still doubted that the visions were real. But, I concluded, they were definitely not hallucinations! One night, I'd interacted with a spirit whose face was half red, half black. When I described it to Carlos, he said, "That's *Shakim*"—an ancient archetypal Amazonian being. I was amazed to see such figures during initiations, since I had no experience with Shuar cosmology. Clearly, the visions were coming from somewhere other than my own unconscious.

My physical senses were heightened, as were my nonphysical ones. Spirits spoke in nonverbal language and showed me their meaning through symbols. So much of what I saw made me question my sanity. I didn't feel like a crazy person, but I thought maybe the universe was more bizarre than I could handle.

Carlos didn't appreciate my need to understand the invisible, non-ordinary world. The questions I had did not occur to him. My logical, categorical mind had no corresponding intellectual muscle in Carlos; his mode of thinking was completely different from mine. What our civilized society calls animism and dismisses without investigation was a hard fact for him. Spirit energy was behind all physical forms. The experiences I thought supernatural were to him an expression of the natural world. My questions about what was real or not real were meaningless to him.

At times, I wondered why I personally had to go to the edge, and why Carlos insisted on teaching me and pushing me. Why couldn't I just be healed and leave everything else alone? Not everyone had to peer into the abyss to find things out. But I knew that in this great struggle I was receiving hard-earned gifts. It seemed now that this was as important to me as being healthy.

I didn't know why I was learning so much so fast or why Carlos was teaching me his techniques. Maybe he wasn't sure why himself. Sometimes I almost forgot about being sick because Carlos got me so interested and excited about everything else. *Warrior,* he'd called me when I'd first come into the jungle. Carlos was preparing me, but I didn't yet know what for.

One day, after we had spent the morning in the jungle, Carlos said, "Prepare for a ritual tonight. I am going to work on Tia."

I had no idea Tia was sick. She didn't, or wouldn't, speak Spanish to me. She worked like a dog, seldom seeming to rest, and it was hard to imagine her, or any of the Shuar women I had met, complaining about anything.

Carlos pronounced that the ceremony had to take place somewhere on the river far away from the house. That meant that Mauro and I had to lug all of Carlos's supplies out to the site. Jorge manned the boat to take us there, but he refused to do any lifting.

Carlos had packed several bundles of rocks, crystals, leaf and condor feather fans, his ceremonial clothes, necklaces, bottles of aguardiente, medicines, half gallon containers of ayahuasca, blankets, bottled water, obsidian stones, his altar cloth, packages of herbs, knives, machetes, oil lanterns, two violins, drums, and the *tumank*— a one-stringed instrument made from a thin bowed branch and wire. Each ritual item was separately wrapped in layers of red cloth, and Mauro and I had to carry them all with the utmost care.

Carlos, Mauro, Jorge, and I landed on one of the countless nameless islands in the Pastaza, a white sandy place with high grassy dunes at its center. One could get lost in the tall grasses— but not for long. The island wasn't that big. There was the constant sound of waves slapping the sandy shore.

Mauro and I waded back and forth from the canoe several times unloading, while Carlos was busy checking in with the local spirits, finding the best place to set up. Jorge sat in the boat and waited for Carlos. They were going back to fetch more supplies at the house. But before Carlos left, he set Mauro and me the task of gathering firewood. He wanted a twenty-foot-high bonfire for the evening ritual. He showed us where to set it up. It seemed insane to make such a giant fire, but Carlos was adamant. I had learned that he was very specific with details, and his requests almost always seemed over the top. Things had to be as he had envisioned them or as they were told to him by the spirits.

Mauro and I hauled the bundled equipment that had been left on the shore and stashed it near where the bonfire would be. Then we searched along the water's edge and through the grass for driftwood. We were at it for a couple of hours, mostly split up from each other. We dragged in branches and logs ten feet long. There was a surprising amount of dead wood, but not many trees on the island. I figured the branches and trunks must have been washed up when the mighty river flooded.

When Mauro and I had collected an enormous pile that we agreed was more than enough wood, Carlos, Jorge, and Jaime (the city *andino* with the ponytail and black marble eyes) arrived—with yet more equipment! We helped unload the boat and lug the stuff to the fire site.

By this time it must have been three in the afternoon. Carlos had returned refreshed and animated. He directed Jaime to collect heavy stones, slabs really; then he turned to Mauro and me. "Look, you two, we need more wood. Get going. There's a lot more to do today besides get firewood."

"No way, Carlos," I said. "We have plenty of wood. Look at this pile! Besides, I want some water to drink and not just a tiny sip."

He looked at me mildly and handed me a bottle, and I drank a cupful of water. I'd deal with the nausea later when the medicine hit me that night. Right then I wanted satisfaction. I sat down. Carlos went to grab my arm. "Come on, Margarita. Don't be that way," he said.

I bolted up and ran into the grass. I kept running. That seemed to give Carlos a signal that I should be chased. I ran deeper into the shelter of the tall grass. Then Mauro got into the action. By this time, I was hidden somewhere far from them, keeping very quiet. I could hear their laughter in the distance. They decided to split up and flush me out. Thrashing through the grass, they found me at the same time, bent down in my hiding place. The two of them tugged on my arms and dragged me out. I fought the whole way to escape their grasp, but they just laughed at me. I was pissed off, and this made them enjoy it all the more. I dug in my heels, but it didn't stop them. We were down by the beach by this time.

"Let me go," I said. "Come on, enough." I realized that they were dragging me into the river. "*Enough!*" I cried. "Stop it!"

Both of them were practically giddy with the fun they were having. They grabbed me under my arms and legs and swung me into the river. I landed with a great splash, coughing and sputtering from the bracing cold and the river water I had swallowed. I came bounding out, soaking wet. I wrung water out of my hair and clothes. Carlos and Mauro began to run like grasshoppers, zigzagging and hopping.

"Mauro, let's get Carlos," I yelled. Mauro tackled Carlos. Soon, I was on him too. We pulled Carlos by his feet, which wasn't hard to do, as he was weak with laughter. In minutes the three of us were in the water, dunking one another and laughing uproariously. Carlos moaned that his watch was probably ruined. I just pushed his head underwater.

We all emerged from the river dripping. "Come on," said Carlos. "I'll help get the last of the wood with you."

We went back into the grass to gather wood. Soon Mauro was beside me.

"I want to show you something," he said. I wondered if this was another prank. I followed him along the edge of the grassy swath. About a hundred feet away from where I had been gathering wood, Mauro pointed down. There was an undulating trail about twelve inches wide and an inch deep in the sand.

"What's that?" I asked.

"I'm pretty sure this is the path of a great snake," said Mauro, so excited he was dancing around. "This is a good sign."

We followed the trail for about sixty yards until it disappeared into the water. Carlos came over to investigate the markings. "Yes," he said. "A very large anaconda. It is a fresh spoor. She must have just slipped into the water. Let's see if we can find her."

Carlos slid into the water up to his chest. He'd lived on river-banks his entire life and he didn't equate swimming toward an anaconda, at least in this instance, with danger. He dove down several times, then surfaced and shook water from his hair. The snake was somewhere in the area, but Carlos couldn't find it.

I knew many of the locals were terrified of the giant reptile, which had been known to attack and devour their children. A large anaconda can have two-inch-long razor-sharp teeth to grab hold of its prey. Its body has hundreds of powerfully joined muscles that can crush life from a man in minutes. Native people made offerings to the snake. Should an anaconda take up residence in one's territory, one behaved with reverence—and extreme caution.

"This is a sign from the *Tsunqui*, the spirit of the waters," said Carlos. "We will have a powerful ceremony tonight."

CHAPTER EIGHT

The Ghost Child

By now it was around five o'clock. My clothes and hair had dried as much as they were going to dry, which was not much; we were in lowland jungle near sea level, where the humidity hovered above 90 percent year-round. Jaime, Carlos, Mauro, and I heaved heavy boulders and flat rocks to make a four-foot-high altar near the bonfire, about forty feet from the water's edge. There was still plenty to do, and I gave up hope of going back to Jorge's to change clothes or rest.

After we got the altar built, I helped Carlos set up his ritual paraphernalia. Soon people would be arriving in boats for the ceremony. In an instant, it was night.

I saw light swinging on the water. About fifteen villagers disembarked from two canoes manned by Jorge and one of his sons. Tia, wrapped in a blanket, was in the lead boat with her husband. The rest of the people were new to me.

Carlos was prepared to perform healings on the villagers, especially Tia, who was having trouble with her hips. The ceremony had been called in her honor. Tia was the first to drink the natem. Then the villagers lined up to drink the medicine that Carlos carefully dispensed. Jorge drank too, the first time I had seen him do so. Prayers, songs, and orations were made. After finishing my cupful of medicine, I moved away from the others, who had settled down on blankets and were huddled near the bonfire. The ayahuasca was an especially strong brew. It was more bilelike in taste, and thicker. That meant it was more concentrated.

I stood alone at the water's edge. The waves lapped against the sand. I waited and watched, marveling at the Milky Way. The liquid blackness of the river reflected the distant suns. Suddenly, searing cold rose through my body. It had begun. The stars streaked across the sky, pulling me along with them.

I had trouble standing and girded myself, bracing my legs. Stars breathed and pulsated, coming close and then receding. The closer the stars, the louder the buzzing grew in my ears. It was as if the earth were a gigantic drone of swarming bees. Then the earsplitting humming blinked off. Silence. The roar came on again and again. I covered my ears but the sound swept me once again up into the sky. I landed. Below me the earth rumbled. I could feel the rippling quakes under my feet and I surfed the tremors. I felt nauseous and shaky, and I wanted to throw up. Jorge appeared. His broad fleshy face caused me to growl at him.

"Let's go. You need to be with the group," he said.

I shook my head. He went to take my arm. I refused to budge. His eyes were gargantuan.

"Get back, Jorge. Stay away from me!" I snarled. I had to be alone. Jorge left, but I saw him run over to Carlos, presumably to complain about me. However, Carlos must not have been worried at my disappearance, as no one bothered me for some time.

Later, I heard my name as if from a great distance. The voice became louder and louder.

"Margarita!" Carlos shouted. "*Ven. Ven aca.*" Come. Come here.

I made my way unsteadily toward him. The horrendous

intensity I had experienced at the water's edge slowly abated. People huddled on blankets between the altar of stones and the raging fire. Carlos was bent over a patient. I saw in the flickering firelight that it was Tia.

"Margarita, come here. I want you to help me," Carlos said. "Watch me and learn. Take the shiri-shiri leaves and fan Tia. Do it rapidly, with as much energy as you can."

I fanned furiously and the shiri-shiri took on a movement of its own. I looked at my arm. It was consciously doing as it had been instructed. There was a brain inside it! Every few minutes Carlos would move around Tia, looking for an entry point. I watched as he worked on her hips and abdomen, pressing and prodding. Another part of me was watching from a distant place.

Carlos looked Tia over, seeing something apparent only to his eyes. He attacked, plunging his fingertips into an area that attracted him. Tia screamed. He was manic and concentrated at the same time.

Carlos grabbed for a bucket. Tia retched into it.

"Please, no more," Tia begged. But he did not stop, and she continued to vomit.

He whispered gently to her, "*Calmate. Tranquillo.*" Then he sang. He straddled her, pressing on her ovaries, rubbing them in a circular motion. She wept.

Her shirt was off. Carlos moved to lower her skirt so that he could work more in the groin area. He looked like he was kneading dough.

"Keep fanning and observe, Margarita."

Then Carlos put my hand on Tia's uterus. I felt something like a wave of disjointed energy coming from the spot. It had a temperature sensation to it, but I found it difficult to tell whether it was hot or cold. It was something different than the way temperature usually feels to the sense of touch.

Carlos turned Tia over and felt around her back. He dug his

hand into the side of her head and she moaned. He crossed down to her backside, where he again kneaded deeply into her upper hips and the socket where the hipbone meets the pelvis. Then he turned her over and dug into pressure points on her lower stomach. Tears streamed from her eyes.

Carlos sat her up and handed me rattles. I passed them over Tia's uterus slowly and shook hard. I was shocked to see something rise out of her body. It was a small, beautiful girl, about two years old, with fine features and curly hair, and it flew out of Tia's womb! The child looked at Carlos and me and then sailed off into the bonfire, where she disintegrated. Tia groaned, stunned and exhausted.

Carlos blew tobacco smoke on Tia's navel, chest, and head. He knelt with his legs akimbo, on either side of her, and cupped his hands around her head. He was singing. Then he lifted his right arm, his palm open to the sky, and implored the Great Spirit for power. He blew forcefully into the crown of her head, filling her with healing energy.

When the healing was complete, Tia turned on her side and slept. I moved on with Carlos and helped him with others. I stayed by his side working with him until dawn.

Al fin—the sun had risen some hours past. A very tired Mauro and I carried Carlos's wrapped medicine bundles to the waiting canoe. Most of the villagers had already been taken back to shore. Jorge, Tia, Mauro, Carlos, Jaime, and I climbed aboard to go back to Jorge's compound.

Breakfast was brief. Finally, everyone left the kitchen except Carlos, Tia, and me. Tia patted me shyly on the back and told Carlos how good she felt. Then she occupied herself with the cooking hearth, piles of food, and dirty dishes in her kitchen. Guinea pigs zigzagged underfoot. I zeroed in on Carlos. "I want to know about that ghost we saw last night."

Carlos replied, "Tia lost a young girl whom she has mourned for decades. The spirit of her child, who died at the age of two, was trapped in her womb. She caused the problems with Tia's hips and uterus. When I released the child so that she could travel into the Universal, I healed Tia."

I was stunned at this solution to a medical problem. Was it psychological? I knew what I had seen. If what had happened was psychological, was it in Tia's head? Then how could I see it? Or Carlos? Did Tia see it too? What *was* it we saw? These questions felt like unsolvable riddles and I knew Carlos was not going to be much help when it came to providing the kind of rational explanations I craved. I tried another tack.

"Why did you want my help with Tia and your other patients?" I said. "I felt ill prepared for the task. I don't really understand much of what you did. But by watching you work, I saw things you were seeing. My body, my arms, my hands seemed to know exactly what to do."

"Now that you no longer need healing, you will help me take care of others who are sick."

My eyebrows went up. Had he really said what I thought he had?

"What did you say?"

"Margarita, you are healed. You no longer have the black smoke trapped in your heart. The sickness has left you."

I was startled by Carlos's pronouncement. I began to cry. From joy. Relief. Fear. Exhaustion. Rage. *Healed and worth the price,* I thought.

"There is a deeper purpose for you coming here, Margarita," Carlos said.

"What is the reason I am here, other than to be cured?"

"Do you remember when we lay on the earth in the jaguar forest in Guatemala?" Carlos asked. This was after our ayahuasca journey at Tikal when I met Carlos for the first time. We'd spent an hour lying on the jungle floor holding hands, listening to jaguars coughing. Carlos had picked an old Ceiba tree for us to lie under. The ground beneath was softened by leaves and pine needles, cool on my skin. "Why do you think I have been teaching you about plants? Why do you think I have been having you and Mauro set up the ceremonies? Why do you suppose you are here, Margarita?"

"To be healed?"

"No!" Carlos was emphatic. "That is only a part of your purpose in being here with me. *Nunqui*, the Earth Mother, married us that day as we lay under the big tree in the forest of Tikal. She formed a bond between us. I thought it was strange because I didn't know you. But I knew we should be together. Now I understand why." Carlos looked me straight in the eye. "The sickness of the earth, the sickness of the tribes, and the sickness in our bodies is linked. Nunqui wants you to help me in my work. She wants you to heal the people and the land with me."

CHAPTER NINE

Petroleros

I wanted to do what Carlos asked—help the sick indigenous people. I'd seen poverty. I'd seen land that was dry and useless from logging. Carlos's words had a profound effect on me and I wanted to join him in his *lucha*, his fight.

My time in the jungle and my work with Carlos and the medicine had opened me up. I began to experience deep feelings of sympathy and compassion. I acutely felt others' suffering during healings, as I had felt Tia's. The awakening of my empathic nature was part of the way that Carlos had healed me. It coincided with his immense compassion and empathy. His mission was simple, and because it was so single-minded, it was extremely powerful. He told me that he had been called by God to help people who were suffering.

"Healing is my mission," said Carlos. "That is my work and my purpose. Each person, each being, each culture, and each nation are a mystery, a world. So it is important to ask, how does one honor each? It is with love. All sicknesses are healed with much love. One has to honor Spirit. How can one honor Spirit? With Love. If you give a lot of love to the patient, if you are giving them a lot of energy, the love that comes from you comes from a spiritual love that is inside you. The Spirit that is flooding you with energy is that which heals. I am here to do God's work."

We finished an ayahuasca ritual at six in the morning that last day at Jorge and Tia's. By seven o'clock I had packed my gear. Tia was up but we had no time for boiled plantains so we quickly hugged good-bye. I was going back to the United States.

Carlos, Mauro, and I left camp with the same group of Indians we had entered with a month earlier. We trekked out of the jungle. It had rained and the temperature had fallen into the forties. (It can get cold in the jungle at night.) My teeth were chattering, my clothing was wet, and we were all exhausted. A truck Jorge had arranged for when he went to town the previous day met us at the end of the dirt road and carried us to Puyo.

In town people were frantic. An Amazonian Quechua office, an indigenous political base, had been bombed. As I waited on the street I spoke with the Quechua from Sarayacu, an interior jungle land that can be reached only by canoe or air from Puyo. They told me that they had been facing persecution for years.

The conflict between the indigenous people and development supporters centered around oil. The incursion of the *petroleros* (oil drillers) in the Amazon sparked conflicts with the native peoples, who wanted to preserve the land, the animals, and their homes. Carcinogenic wastes from oil extraction and breaks in pipelines had contaminated rivers, streams, and ground water in the lands north of Puyo. The native population had been afflicted with chronic and acute illnesses, including cancer.

President Gutierrez's government, in power at the time of the bombing in Puyo, maintained that the indigenous peoples owned the land, but that the ground six inches *under* the topsoil was government property. The military accompanied the petroleros into the field to enforce cooperation. I was told that tribal chiefs of Sarayacu had been murdered. Contaminated food had been purposefully sent into their jungle communities, killing mostly women and children.

I heard these nightmarish stories while eating a stew of wild pig in the Native restaurant run by a Sarayacu family who were known for their activism. They had been instrumental in uniting tribes in the Amazon against the government and petroleros. Spears and blowguns hung on the restaurant walls, evoking another era, along with photos of aboriginal families. The family told me some Sarayacu members had been ambushed and kidnapped. An attorney representing the Sarayacu people was assaulted and threatened at gunpoint. The attacks were all attributed to Sarayacu's opposition to oil exploration.

Today, the Sarayacu people have police stationed outside their new office in Puyo. Seven years and $10 million into the project, the oil company hasn't yet been able to start drilling, but many people have died.

After lunch, Jaime took off to rent a van to take Carlos, Mauro, and me back to Quito. The others we had traveled with dispersed. We said our good-byes to the locals and headed for the mountains. Carlos was supposed to be taking me back to the city; from there I would make arrangements for my flight. But he had other plans.

"Our journey is not quite over," he said. "I've prepared a special ceremony in the mountains for you."

"Tonight? Can we rest first?" I was happy to be able to do one more ceremony before leaving, but I dreaded it at the same time.

"Yes, we're going to a special place in the Andes to take in the elements," he said. "You'll be able to relax and quickly become renewed."

Jaime drove north along the mountainous spine with its treacherous turns. Up, up, and up we went, out of the reaches of the

Amazon basin, into the Andes. The air got cooler. Carlos and Mauro
were passed out in the backseat, while I sat up front, clutching the
dashboard with white knuckles. Small houses hung precariously to
the terraced hillsides. The vistas were immense, a startling change
after my weeks in the close confines of the jungle. As we forged
through Andean passes, we saw the active, spewing volcano
Tungurahua, 16,456 feet high. Ash plumed in the air, and it had
covered much of the outlying villages. Jaime told me that it was
causing damage to the land and farm animals. Children were having
trouble breathing. Fortunately, there had been no deaths. The
ground was powdered an indiscriminate gray. I found it both
exciting and slightly unnerving that *El Comercio*, the main news-
paper in Quito, in place of a weather report on the front page, listed
what each active volcano in Ecuador was doing that day.

The four of us arrived late afternoon in Baños, a touristy town
where people could take trekking adventures with guides going river
rafting, going to an ayahuasca ceremony in the jungle, or going to
places with names like Devil's Drop. I laughed at the idea of pack-
aged tourist adventures. I wouldn't sign up for an eco-tour designed
for a group experience with an unknown guide. Carlos was guiding
me, and his fight was for the things that really mattered.

CHAPTER TEN

The Boiling Waterfall

The next morning, after a night in a tattered hotel in Baños, we were on the road again in the direction of Cayambe, an 18,997-foot volcano with a bright glacier on the summit. Its sides were pitted with deep striations caused by massive mud and lava flows, though the mountain had not erupted since the eighteenth century. Cayambe is the only place in the world where the equator crosses the summit of glaciated mountains. Carlos called it the mountain of white magic.

"When we are healing patients we will bring the pure energy from this place into our patient," he said. "We use the power of Cayambe." I was curious how it was possible to bring a mountain's energy into a person, and I wondered if I'd be able to learn how to do it. Carlos had shown me the peak of Sangay when we were outside Puyo. That was the mountain of black magic that was used by *brujas*, or witches, to bring in dark energy to cause illness and even death.

For the next several hours the car wound its way up the side of a peak in the vicinity of Cayambe. Rocky, snow-covered spires in the background were twenty, forty miles in the distance. At Carlos's command, Jaime stopped the car on a desolate plateau. We were in the *páramo*, the ecosystem located in the high elevations between the upper forest line, 10,000 feet, and the permanent snow line, about 16,500 feet. The vegetation consisted of tussock grasses and dwarf shrubs. There were valleys and lakes in the distance that had been formed by glaciers. Below us were bogs, shrublands, and forest patches. We were about sixty miles from Quito, in a rugged, isolated region with no people or homesteads in sight.

We began walking toward the summit on a narrow path that wound along steep ravines. The path skirted large haphazardly placed stones that looked like they had been dashed into the ground. I wondered if they had come from volcanoes that had exploded thousands of years ago.

We came to an outlook. I felt wobbly from the altitude; we must have been well above 10,000 feet. The wind was gusting at 60 miles an hour or more. My breathing was heavy, the air thin, and my legs barely moved. I wanted to crawl, grabbing on to stones so I wouldn't be blown from the mountaintop to the valley below. I felt small, useless, and forlorn in the bleak, uninhabited land, as if I had reached the very end of the earth.

After the 90-degree temperatures in the rainforest, the dry icy wind was searing. I had brought gloves from New York, thin ones that I thought I might need in the jungle to handle dangerous things—what, I didn't know—and I pulled them out of my pack to cover my hands. I was not built for this terrain, but then again, I thought, who was?

Snow covered the ground. I felt the biting cold, and I feared I was getting frostbite on my hands and feet. But in spite of feeling so utterly unsheltered and hopeless on the bleak face of the pinnacle, I sensed that the mountain was alive.

"Here Mother Earth is known as *Pachamama*," Carlos said. "The mountains are infused with powerful nature spirits. The ancient Quechua beliefs prevail in this remote region. This is home to the great condor."

Carlos prayed with his arms outstretched. "The mountain lives and feels. The most direct source of healing, divine power, is concentrated on the mountain because the purest energies come from the high pinnacles of earth.

"One is closest to *Uwinsut*, the God of Creation, who lives on the mountaintops. We show great respect for the life force here because it permeates everything and nourishes the lives of people, animals, and plants. We call on its force and focus the energy into the patient.

"Breathe in, absorb the purity and refreshment of the air and snow. Now you must take in the intense cold and take this power into you. The power of *Mayai*, the fresh, virginal breath of life."

I sucked in my breath, inhaling the frigid air.

Carlos and Mauro played a tune on panpipes to the deities of the place. We left tobacco offerings as a sign of respect. Carlos picked up a piece of raw obsidian from the ground and gave it to me, saying, "Stones contain concentrated life force. They communicate and offer their powers to those with faith. We are to pray here and relay our greatest faith. We are here to make a wish."

What was my wish? I could sense that I was at the beginning of something huge. I wished that now that I had been taken apart, I would be put back together in a wholesome way. I prayed for the love, sensitivity, and grace to accept the will of the Divine, and I gave thanks for my life.

When our ritual was done, we drove down the mountain. Still high in altitude, we got out of the car to climb into a valley where Carlos showed us a secret passageway into the earth. The corridor was invisible to the naked eye; I could not see it. But the area around the "mother mountain" looked like an old Flemish painting, a Bruegel, in which more perspective than was possible was contained in the view. The green pastures sloped and undulated;

there were endless knolls and prominences of brilliant green. Everything was so neat and clean; it had not yet been altered by human encroachment.

Back in the car, we descended again and passed through a portal where the ecosystem transformed from alpine to jungle patched with cloud forests. I spied dirt roads like capillaries disappearing behind the hills. We passed by several villages before we came to a sign for Baeza and Lago Agrio. We took the road to the Papallacta thermal baths.

At the sacred pools, boiling water bubbled up from the ground. The phenomenon that produced the scorching waters was called *Caldera*—the Boiler. The once active volcano had created rivulets of magma that settled near the surface of the earth at Papallacta. The hot water in the pools ran from the magma fissures up and onto the ground. There were dozens of different natural rock pools in the area. Wounded Incan warriors had once come to these curative waters for healing.

Carlos, Mauro, Jaime, and I entered the pool site for a nominal fee. The place was a clean, well-developed Ecuadorian resort spot, the parking lot partially filled with cars. I watched ten or so families, well-to-do by Ecuadorian standards, swim in a large and temperate pool that looked like a swimming pool in the States. The kids laughed, splashing water at one another. There were no other gringos, but no one paid attention to my presence. I entered a stall to put on a bathing suit. My skin was goose-pimpled as I came out: It was 65 degrees and windy. We were probably at 11,500 feet.

There were several pools of varying size, although Carlos, Mauro, Jaime, and I centered around two, the hottest and the coldest. These pools were not particularly large, though one was thirty or forty feet in length, deep enough for me to submerge completely, and virtually empty but for us.

It was curiously funny to see Carlos and Mauro in bathing suits. I expected them to be naked, which seemed more suited to their natures. Did they borrow the suits? I wondered. The costume looked normal on Jaime, who was a city *andino*. Carlos wore flip-flops and had a towel slung over his shoulder. He looked like any of the men taking the baths—just another worker. I wondered at his chameleon nature. It felt odd being with everyday folks, with those who had no inclination to absorb the spirit of the waters.

But this was no holiday dip we were taking. As we all stood looking out over the steaming spring-fed water encased in natural stone and manmade rock, Carlos began the lessons. "Your body must receive benefits from the two great powers," Carlos said. "Heat and cold must claim you to remove all the sickening sweat from your body. It is time for us to take in the healing waters. The volcanic heat that spews forth from the mountain, the heart of Our Mother, will enter you."

I stuck my toe into the first of the pools. The water was scalding and I had to slowly submerge. I thought it was all I could bear, but, as I was to learn, I didn't really know yet what scalding was or how much my body could take. Carlos edged me, in time, under a waterfall where the water was actually boiling in spots.

Carlos swam under the falls and was gone. Suddenly he surfaced, took my hand, and pushed me under the gushing cascade. Inside was a misty turquoise cave in the rock. The air steamed. My skin was lobster-red, so I made my way out of the cave to where the water felt cooler. Then I followed Carlos in and out of the cave. We were the only ones who entered this place. It was far too hot for comfort. Jaime would disappear frequently, and Mauro would take in the extreme waters of the pools in stretches, and then he'd take a break to girl-watch. I don't remember either Jaime or Mauro going under the falls.

"Harness your will," Carlos said, "and the power of your mind to be able to take the extreme temperatures." He told me to follow him into another bubbling pool and commanded that I jump in. It was heart-stopping cold. My teeth felt like they were being bored with a dentist's drill. The feeling went all the way from the tips of my toes to the top of my skull.

Carlos had me immerse myself in the scalding pool and then go lie in a pool of freezing water. Then back into the hot pool—on and on.

"You will learn to cool your body temperature by internal refrigeration," he said, "or increase the fire inside you while in the snow."

After several hours, my skin was wrinkly and I was becoming dehydrated. For some reason the baths sucked water out of me. I was also struggling not to get sunburned. Then Carlos decided it was time to eat.

We dressed quickly, turned in our towels, and walked to a local restaurant where we indulged in a feast of flavors with gusto. We ate fried trout and *locro,* a typical Andean soup made with potatoes, cheese, avocado, and milk. I drank an aguardiente that zoomed right into my brain. Then we slept in a hostel nearby until early morning. I slept deeply after the springs.

The next day, after I confirmed my airline reservations, we went to the Equator, which was marked by a painted yellow line on the ground. It was known as *La Mitad del Mundo* (the middle of the world). In a nearby museum, you could watch water flow down three drains in different directions. In the northern and southern hemispheres, it flowed in opposite spirals, clockwise in the north and counterclockwise in the south. On the Equator it flowed straight down. It was also possible to balance an egg on a nail in this place of equilibrium.

I stood with a leg in the northern hemisphere and a leg in the southern hemisphere. What a grand feeling to be on both sides of the earth simultaneously. I yelped with pleasure. It seemed a fitting moment, one that balanced me and gave me a sense of completion. I was feeling the stability of rightly weighted scales after going from high to low, hot to cold, physical to psychic, an arduous journey of extremes. Jaime took photos of us walking the line with silly smiles on our faces. I had no idea where the camera came from.

CHAPTER ELEVEN

Woman from the North

My last evening in Ecuador, as he had promised, Carlos conducted a ceremony in the Andes at the Temple of the Jaguar. The temple, which a Columbian architect had designed for rituals, was about twenty miles outside of Quito in a cold, windswept place. The walls were sculpted from rock in curious heights and outlandish shapes. Large glass windows shaped like equilateral triangles dotted the exterior. Chimneys loomed in the night sky. Leading to the building were stones cut into the shape of the prints of giant jaguar paws.

The inside of the structure was permeated with dark red. Mosaics of thirty-foot snakes lined the walls. The central area contained a hearth with a fire already roaring. Indians were gathered, some of whom I recognized from the jungle. They had been waiting for hours for our arrival, and they ran to Carlos with children in their arms or hobbled to him with sick, agonized faces.

Carlos quickly but carefully set up his paraphernalia. The altar was covered as usual with the red felt cloth decorated with hand-embroidered condors, eagles, jaguars, mountains, and magical symbols. Obsidian and purple grandmother crystals were placed on the altar, along with a half gallon of ayahuasca. Carlos and the altar were on an elevated platform, like overseers.

The ceremony began with a plea for the suffering, the hungry, and the orphans of the world. One by one the poor climbed up to Carlos to receive the spirit of the plant. I was at the tail end of the line.

I was taken quickly by the medicine and began to sing. Or scream. Sounds came out of me that I hope never to hear again. Soon Mauro was vocalizing too and the room seemed full of demons and chaos. Carlos quickly took control. A jaguar appeared and Carlos sicced the cat on us. It sped through the room, eating human cries. Then Carlos began treatments.

A few hours passed, and I found I had to get outside to pee. I didn't want to leave the confines of the room, which felt protective, but I was desperate. I walked outside scared. I was awkwardly appraising the raised jaguar stones in the dark when I tripped hard and sprained my ankle. My pants were torn at the knee and blood seeped out. They were the last undamaged pair I had brought with me, the clothes I had planned to fly home in.

I continued on, frightened, and made it to the outhouse. I quickly closed the heavy hand-hewn door and rushed over to the toilet, which was both a surprise and a luxury; I'd expected a hole in the ground. When I finished and came out of the stall, I became aware of small neon green monsters with ferociously sharp teeth closing in on me. I tried to brush past them, the guardians of the door to the bathroom and my freedom, as quickly as I could. But they had locked the door from the outside. I pulled with all my might again and again, but I could not escape. They swiped at me, chomping their vicious jaws, and I batted them away with a broom handle. I screamed but no one came to my rescue. There was one way out—a window. I stood on the toilet seat. The monsters told me they'd be waiting outside for me.

It was so dark I had no idea how far the drop was, but I was being attacked so I jumped, dropping through a thorn bush and what felt like far too much space. I hit the ground, landing on the ankle I had sprained. I rolled into a ball. Tears sprang from my eyes and the green ones yelled, "Hah! We've done you harm, and we're coming to get you!" They were attacking me because they had the opportunity since I'd removed myself from the protective circle Carlos created in the Jaguar Temple. Not all the creatures one met during rituals were good ones.

I bounded upward, trying to run. I crawled and dragged my leg in the long journey back to the safe environs of the ceremony. The creatures snapped like hyenas, but they did not follow me on the jaguar path.

Just as I passed through the door and breathed a sigh of relief, Carlos called to me to meet him on the elevated platform. The group was on the floor, circled around Carlos and the altar. I limped slowly toward Carlos, acutely aware of the pain in my ankle and leg. I wondered if it would feel worse when I was off the medicine, but I figured Carlos knew what had happened and was going to produce his magic and fix me.

Instead he pulled up a chair next to his and asked me to sit at his right hand—an unheard-of honor, Mauro whispered in my ear. Mauro sat on Carlos's left side. Carlos was straight. Serious. Immobile. The three of us faced an audience of Native peoples.

Carlos began a speech. He ritually acknowledged me in front of the group, then presented me with a spear, a ceremonial necklace, and a large crystal he used for healing. "These powerful objects I give to you," he said. He looked out at the assembly. "This woman from the North has come to help the indigenous people, the down-trodden, the sick and poor. She is here to combat the sickness and humiliation our people have endured since the arrival of the Spanish. She is a spiritual woman and a warrior for the *pueblos originarios*. Original people. The Great Spirit has brought her here."

Then he turned to me. "My son Mauro and I prepared this spear and necklace for the commencement of your birth into a new life. Each embellishment on these sacred objects was prayed over and massive energy was wound into them. Making these ritual pieces required over a week's time."

I gazed at the wonderful things he had made with his hands for me, holding them with great care. "Thank you, Carlos; you honor me. I accept these things with reverence and responsibility for their use."

He placed an intricate necklace over my head. It was designed from the small seeds that designated the Shuar people, the Eye of the Deer seeds, and the red and black seeds of *Shakim*, who was the spirit of the plants and the forest.

"The red and the black represent the two spirits or forces that control the universe. One is positive energy, or light, and the other is negative energy, the dark. Both forces are gods. Both invincible. We only know one of these powers—light. The light of obscurity we don't know, but it is a light that is the opposite of the light we see.

"These powerful tools will protect you when you are attacked by malevolent spirits. Should I not be with you, take this spear and raise it against the beings that would try to suck your power. This will always work against them, but your intention must be formidable. In the future you will wear the ceremonial necklace during ritual work."

Carlos faced the people and said, "This woman is an *embajadora*, an ambassador, and together we will build a bridge between the North and the South. Let us give thanks to the Great Spirit that our worlds may be united for the greater good of all."

The ritual was complete. Many participants left the temple; others slept as we gathered our things and packed them in the car. Jaime drove us to the airport. In half an hour I would be in the check-in line with my passport and backpack. Before we parted, Carlos recounted again the vision that we would work together to heal the sick. "Our work is not yet finished, Margarita," he said. "You must continue your journey on the Red Path."

"Carlos, I am leaving for New York now."

"Yes, Margarita. But you will be back. We will build a hospital together in the jungle. We will treat the poor and suffering. Your cancer is gone. You no longer have that inside you."

When I could finally muster words, I said, "I can't tell you how much everything here, everything you've done, everything I've gone through has meant to me. I have such joy deep in my heart."

Carlos told me that the most important work was ahead of us. I had the work of integrating what I had learned in the jungle, incorporating it into my life, and I needed to turn my service toward helping others who were less fortunate.

Carlos had invested himself in the journey I'd undertaken into my own personal, intimate healing, and that moved me. I had been honored to assist him with Tia and his patients. With a flood of tears, I realized how profoundly all that Carlos and I had endured together had transformed me. I hugged Carlos, Mauro, and Jaime. We had had such an incredible voyage together.

I couldn't conceive of a more fulfilling life than helping the sick and poor. And I wanted desperately to continue working with Carlos, to keep learning, to journey further along the Red Path.

But that feeling was accompanied by dangers and anxieties. I had come to Ecuador to heal myself, and suddenly here I was being cast in a new role, enlisted for a spiritual adventure in a tradition that had remained pretty much unchanged since the Stone Age. What Carlos was telling me was that my destiny was completely outside the bounds of my well-to-do life as a middle-class American woman. It was ridiculous, impossible, and thrillingly seductive.

As my plane took off and circled Quito in the early-morning sky, I could see to the east, where the big mountains fell down into a vast dominion of green, the endless jungle stretching away into Brazil. I knew the direction I wanted my life to take, but I had no idea how to make it work with my family or career. I was staring at the crossroads of my life.

PART TWO

APPRENTICESHIP

CHAPTER TWELVE

Dangerous Nonsense

As the cab pulled up to my home, Gray Cottage, in the Hudson Valley of upstate New York, I felt as though I was arriving in a picture postcard. Red geraniums stood in stone planters on either side of the white front door of the house, a two-story clapboard structure built in 1829. Those same flowers, native to Ecuador, had reached my chest there, blossoming like giant bushes. The house looked empty. But my husband's old Mercedes was parked in the drive.

The front door swung open and there stood Miles, my husband of twenty years. He wore a blue oxford shirt that matched his eyes, and his golden hair curled over his ears. He was a handsome man, six feet tall and muscular, a merchant seaman in his twenties and now a respected and talented avant-garde filmmaker. He was professorial, but not academic like others in his department at the college where he taught.

We embraced as the taxi driver removed my bag from the trunk of the car. Miles grabbed my backpack and looked me up and down. I stood there in front of the house with him, a different woman. I was thinner, but that wasn't all.

"How was your trip?" Miles asked. "You doing okay?"

"Good. I'm fine. Carlos said my cancer is gone," I said, already beginning to doubt myself. I hated that.

"That's great, but don't get your expectations too high. You've got an appointment with the doctor next week."

I frowned. Was he chastising me? But I continued: "Ecuador was great. It was exotic and enlivening. Beautiful. I don't know how to describe what happened there."

Miles seemed interested in me, glad that I was home. But he hadn't wanted to take the time to drive to the airport to pick me up.

"It's been a long journey," I said. "We had a stopover in Bogota and then Miami. Look at me. I'm filthy." I was wearing my ratty jungle clothes.

I was happy to see him, but I felt muted. I had been so absorbed in the excitement surrounding my initiations in Ecuador that I hadn't given a thought to a reunion with Miles or the comfort of home. I was full of stories and excitement. But I knew immediately that I could not tell him, really, what had gone on in Ecuador. I didn't think he would understand, and it would reveal too much the person that I had become, the "me" that even I was not yet accustomed to. Perhaps that was the person I had been all along. She had no relation to the woman Miles thought he'd married when we were young artists and free. Over time, a line of experimentation and personal freedom had been drawn in the sand, and now I had stepped beyond it. I was at a loss as to what to do or say.

"I'm in desperate need of a bath and fresh clothes," I said. "How are you? Has Manon called from camp?"

"Things are pretty much the same as when you left. Too much work, but a little time for golf dates. I ate out every night. It was lonely with you gone and Manon away."

I walked into the living room. Two of the cats lay on the leather couch, ignoring me. Our daughter would be home from camp in a week. The dining table was covered with papers, and the pale yellow walls looked like they needed painting again. The room felt small, condensed. Being home felt as if I'd stepped into a time machine. The atmosphere felt lukewarm and old, like entering my grandmother's house as a child, with the smell of Red Daddy's shaving soap and the musty odors trapped in the walls and furniture. The television lit up and spoke like the wizard in Oz, surreal, two-dimensional. I wondered at the action caught in the box. Why didn't people have real adventures?

"I made some chili," Miles said. "I'll heat it while you bathe." He was being kind and thoughtful. I felt a vague, pervading guilt for having gone away. I felt scattered and dispersed, in pieces, and I needed time to coalesce—if that was possible.

I stood in the familiar upstairs bathroom off the bedroom. The bed, the tub, the rug, and the neat bedspread all seemed to mock me with promises of comfort and stability that now seemed not only beside the point, but pointless. I dried my hair with a fresh towel and went downstairs and tried to persuade myself as I ate Miles's chili that the chitchat we managed to maintain about practical matters of the family would get us through this awkward phase.

Later, I walked outside to the great oak tree in the backyard and looked up at it. The long summer evening of these northern latitudes deepened slowly, so unlike the immediate nightfall in the jungle. I had watched the oak over the seasons for years and my fondness for it was one thing that seemed undiminished. The oak had a sense of permanence. Suddenly, I felt bereft. Why didn't it mirror the change within me? Why hadn't it changed as I had? Why had I changed so much? I stood in the grass and cried. *I can't go home again,* I thought. *I've journeyed too far from what I thought I knew.*

In the next few days, Miles and I reestablished a tenuous bond. I found it next to impossible to find my way through my daily routine. I had immense difficulty keeping the checkbook in order, shopping for groceries, driving the car into town. It wasn't incapability. The disconnect that I felt with my old life was rooted in the knowledge that my marriage was no longer working, that in fact it hadn't worked in years. Miles was oblivious. He acted as if our estrangement was natural and ordinary and acceptable. Why did I have to be the one to reveal this painful secret? I pondered long and hard over whether it was crueler to end the marriage or continue. I had no answers, but I felt myself pulling away: My old life and my marriage seemed increasingly remote, and this made me feel very, very sad.

But I was not only struggling with vertigo as I futilely tried to reconnect with my former life. I had an appointment with my doctor for tests and scans that would tell me Carlos was right and my cancer was gone.

The day came in June 2000 and Miles and I boarded a train in Rhinecliff bound for Penn Station. We sat in opposite seats and left the train separately; as I rushed into the subway station, Miles was already buying our tokens. Going up in the hospital elevator, he sighed. The distance between us made me feel weary and sorrowful. I guessed he was feeling the same way. I wanted to connect with him, but I didn't seem to be able to remember how to do that. Time, habit, and complacency had slowly been robbing our love, loosening our bond. Our one commonality seemed to be my illness.

We sat down in the breast cancer center. Miles flicked the pages of a magazine and glanced up at CNN. He was silent, detached, and so was I. I went through the rigmarole of tests. The cold instruments and antiseptic environment were the polar opposite of what I had experienced in Ecuador. And then we waited together in the same attenuated, disconnected state. CNN droned. The fluorescent lights overhead faintly buzzed. The women sitting around us were each lodged in their own private nightmares.

Finally, we were ushered into the inner office to meet with the doctor, a man I'd grown to like and trust and for whom I had a deep respect. He stood in his white coat with an easy, friendly smile. He was the cool, temperate version of Carlos, who seemed a fast flame in comparison. This doctor wanted to ease things for me. It had been a year since I had been diagnosed, and he had seen me through two rounds of surgery; I'd refused the other treatments offered.

"I've looked at the tests," he said. "There's no cancer." I mentioned my trip to South America for treatment.

"Keeping your spirits up is good for you. I'm glad you've been traveling. Whatever works," he said, mildly surprised I was doing so well.

"Is it really over?" I cried.

"Come back in a year and we'll take a look."

Miles stood up. Relief washed over his face. We both pumped the doctor's arm profusely and bounded for the door.

I thought back to Carlos's pronouncement that I was healed. The relief was physical. First I crumpled, and then it was as if I was filled with helium and I could rise like vapor.

I was a buoyant, giddy woman on the train ride home. Miles's mood lightened; he too felt a great weight lift. But then the oddest thing happened when I stepped over the threshold of Gray Cottage. The good news I had just received began to feel like a burden. Now I had a future. And freedom. To do what? It dawned on me that my expectations, ambitions, plans, relationships, sense of belonging, were all blasted. The experiences in South America had healed something in me, but they had shattered my world. I struggled to find a bridge between my life with my family and my other life—my life as Other.

I imagined myself driving over the Rhinecliff Bridge to the other side of the Hudson River. The river was wide and far beneath me, gray with a flat sheen and the solidity of iron. The wind blew and my Honda rocked and swayed. I chugged forward over the long arc of the bridge, willing my car to reach the far bank where the green land resumed and I would be safe, on solid ground. And I would be able to understand the differences between the two sides and everything would make sense to me. The image kept appearing in my mind.

Meanwhile, spirits visited me in my home. Before they arrived I would smell the distinct, slightly sickening odor of ayahuasca cooking. They were calling me back. When I took walks in the forest near the house, I would become "enchanted," lost to time. It was often hours before I remembered that I had to return, that Miles was waiting or that I had plans. Sometimes I saw Carlos in the jungle. Once I saw a deer that talked to me and told me I was on the right path. I kept trying to connect the dots, make a bridge between the Hudson Valley and the jungle, and connect my disparate lives in a meaningful way. I felt like I was losing my mind.

My daughter, Manon, had been away at camp, but I wanted to have a clear head and a firm grasp on my life for her return. She was only fifteen, and I didn't want her to see me so confused and ungrounded. I thought the best way to get my feet back on the ground would be to go back to work, so I went into my studio and tried to turn my thoughts toward composing.

My studio was on the ground floor of our home, surrounded on three sides by windows as old as the house, made of small panes of glass. It looked onto the greenery, a birdbath, and the wildflowers that surrounded the house. The floors, made from wide planks that had been cut over a hundred years ago, were covered by an ancient Afghan rug. The furniture was shabby but somehow comforting. Old newspapers and books on acoustics were sloppily piled on the floor next to my thinking chair. A teacup with a used teabag in it sat next to the computer on my walnut desk. String and percussion instruments were lined up on the shelves—ocarinas, harmonicas, Egyptian three-stringed violins, tambourines, bird whistles, and drums. A B-Series Steinway upright was stacked with a pile of modern music and a Beethoven sonata open on top. Manon, who was a vastly talented pianist, must have been here and played the piece while I was gone. I felt safe in this room.

After my diagnosis, I had buried myself in my work. Music had poured from me. I had been working on sound installations for galleries and museums. I simulated wolf howls with French horns and low-frequency oscillators. I evoked deer calls with strings that played quiet, haunting, slow-moving harmonies. I created whirring, murmuring "moon" sounds and the raining, glistening cries of peacocks, rabbits, and owls. The voices were hidden in the gallery walls, disembodied. Crying from the void. Death vied with the enormous potential of magic and creation. I had written obsessively, urgently. I had also composed music for performances in Eindhoven and 's-Hertogenbosch, Holland. I was back and forth between Europe, New York, and L.A. I ran. I flew. I was on the edge of my life.

Now that flurry of work seemed as remote and insubstantial as everything else. My thoughts revolved around Carlos and my time with him in the Amazon. I was putting something together in my mind. Carlos's ceremonies were alive. Immediate. They were music; they were art, beauty, and healing. I realized that my impulse to work with him had been, in part, an artistic choice. My own music had exemplified an ecstasy that was similar to the freedom Carlos the uwishin maintained. In Carlos's ceremonies, many people experienced the rituals in a personal, ecstatic way. Carlos was the maestro. He brought the divine down to earth. In writing music, I too had been calling the ecstatic, the divine.

While in Ecuador, I had recorded several CDs' worth of Carlos's music. I got up from my chair and put one on the sound system. Hearing the insects, waterfalls, the sounds of birds, and Carlos's voice brought me back to the jungle, as a photograph will bring a memory of a place alive. The music was simple, mesmerizing.

I recalled a night when we sat at the edge of the Puyo River. Carlos had played his violin and tumank. Carlos needed the sound of rushing water to fill his ears. Natural sounds informed the music, he said. They *are* the music.

He always used instruments in the healing ceremonies. These, along with his voice and prayers, were vehicles for calling the healing spirits. When he whistled, an eerie, ethereal sound came from him; his whistling was a pipeline through the portal dimensions.

"As I chant in front of the patient, I chant to the spirits to whom I have dedicated myself," Carlos said. "Then it is not I who is chanting but the spirits, which present themselves and sing through me. I have made a pact with them." His music seemed to flow like water. Natural. Pure. Unconscious. Inspired.

I placed another CD in the changer. It was part of a six-hour ceremony recorded on the banks of the Pastaza. Carlos's prayers and music began. After twenty minutes or so, I heard voices I recognized wailing. The ceremony replayed in my head: I remembered a Shuar from one of the villages near Jorge's vomiting and vomiting until blood oozed from his lips. Carlos had attended him, especially his lungs. The firelight had flickered and the sound of the river rushing had filled my ears. Insects shrilled in patterns moving through the forest.

"Faster, faster," Carlos had said as I worked the fan of condor feathers over the retching, bleeding man.

Miles stood in the doorway. "What is that I'm hearing? Are people throwing up?"

"Yes." I tried to explain what I could barely comprehend myself. "During the healing sessions, people are required to drink a liquid made from freshly collected plants, and it causes them to vomit out toxins and waste." The recording sounded more and more awful. "These are the holy songs that call the spirits of healing," I said.

"Why is there screaming and crying?"

"People hurt physically or emotionally. They're afraid. It's all part of what the healers call cleansing the system."

"Were you taking drugs?" Miles asked.

"No," I said. "I didn't take drugs, but I saw things. I was told certain things." I began to talk about an Indian spirit of the jungle and some poignant moments that had occurred during my time with Carlos. I found myself talking about the sacred things that Carlos and Mauro had made for me. But then I couldn't go on.

Miles stood looking at me from the doorway with an expression that was both skeptical and frightened. I was discovering the uselessness of trying to put into words something fantastically potent, but weirdly inappropriate to speak of to the uninitiated. I didn't think it was a shortcoming that Miles couldn't understand the world I had entered. He didn't have the frame of reference for it. I realized that what had happened to me was utterly incomprehensible to him. What I saw and heard *are* improbable in my culture.

"I don't understand," he said. "What about your music and composing? Why aren't you doing that? Get back to what is important in your life. Why are you even listening to this?"

"I need to come to grips with my experience in the jungle. Everything's gone topsy-turvy. There's too much I've taken in that I need to digest. I can't write music now."

I saw Miles's incredulity. He couldn't understand how I could put myself through exposure to anything so disgusting and ludicrous.

"Your 'adventures' are no more than superstitious nonsense, and dangerous nonsense at that," he said. It angered him that, with familial responsibilities to consider, I'd gone out on this perilous limb. "You've put yourself at risk."

"I'm sorry you feel that way, although I do understand how difficult this is," I said. "I'll not make any excuses, because this is what has happened and I can't change any of it or pretend it doesn't exist."

The silence descended as he stood in the doorway, and we looked at each other, both knowing the horror we were facing—the possibility of losing a twenty-year marriage.

My heart was aching and the pressure to act or not act was enormous. This too, I understood, was a challenge a real warrior would have to confront. At that moment I hated the Red Path because it demanded far too much.

CHAPTER THIRTEEN

Threat of Drought and Famine

Miles and I had hit bottom, and my life was in a complete shambles. Everything had blown up, everything, except my relation to my daughter and a few close friends. Even with Manon home from camp, visions of the jungle continued to haunt me. Then Carlos e-mailed me from an Internet café in Quito.

"It is a pleasure for me to be able to tell you of the pleasant memories you leave in me." He wrote in stately, formal Spanish that he'd learned in missionary school with Silesian priests. "I wish that the path that we have begun will be enriched by your presence once again. I saw you come into the circle during a recent ceremony I conducted in the Jaguar Temple where we made our sacred ritual. You were leading the people. There were many jovial faces. I prayed to the Great Spirit that these visions would come to pass. I saw us healing in North America and here in the jungle. You must return to your studies with me. You must continue what the Great Spirit has entrusted into your hands. A warm embrace and much love. Carlos, *El Jaguar Negro*."

This was the last straw. I was being irresistibly drawn back into

Carlos's web, and I let myself go. I finally admitted that I was like Carlos because my studies in healing were about more than just the healing itself. They were a quest for knowledge, for understanding and a deep relation to God—all those things that for Carlos were paramount. The Red Path was a mission and a duty. It was my life's path, and to turn away from what I had begun would be a betrayal, an impossibility. I wanted more: I wanted to go deeper, higher, faster, farther. And I knew with absolute certainty that working with Carlos, all these things could be. I began to make plans to return to Ecuador.

But I wanted to spend the rest of the summer of 2000 with Manon before she went off to boarding school. It was terribly important to me that she know how much I loved her and no matter what I did, or how much I changed, nothing ever would—or could—change that.

We sat in Manon's room, on her bed, where one of our cats had given birth to kittens a few years earlier. Manon had skipped school that day to watch. The walls were covered with pictures she was fond of, mostly animals. I gave her a hug.

"You know," I began, "as a toddler you were always so tender with all our pets. You never once made them cry by pulling their tails or ears. That's unusual for a two-year-old. Remember when we read *My Family and Other Animals*, by Larry Durrell?"

"We should read it again," Manon said. "That was our favorite book."

"Larry was complaining about his family and how hard it was to get them to understand him and his fascination with animals and the creatures on the island of Crete. Even the scorpions."

"Yeah, I remember."

"Maybe you've felt a bit like Larry in our household lately. Pushed aside, perhaps? Misunderstood?"

She looked and waited for me to continue.

"I'm sorry I wasn't here for you when you went off to camp," I said. "I was so frightened when I got cancer, and I know it scared you too. Sometimes things happen that we have no control over."

"I know, Mom, but why did you have to go away to get well?" She wanted me to justify my behavior in a way that made her feel like she was still the center of my universe—which, of course, she was.

"Please don't condemn me for having gone away," I said. "I didn't do it because I wanted to leave you. I needed to go. I'm better now. I've beaten cancer and I feel more alive."

Manon could see that I seemed happier, that I did feel more alive. But although she didn't say so, I could tell she was thinking, *What about me?* I knew she wanted to believe that love is unconditional and that home never changes. She needed that constancy to feel safe. We all know this about our children and we want to give it to them—as much as we are able. Love is constant, I believe. But everything else shifts.

That month before Manon left for school, we were very close; Miles kept to himself, giving us space. He and I were distant and polite. We treasured our time cooking together. We made pies, lasagna, chocolate mousse, cakes, and more pies. We went shopping, and we listened to lots of music: Beethoven, Penderecki, Lizst, Debussy. Manon was and is an inspired pianist, full of passion and brilliant technique. We discussed phrasing, figured bass, harmonic, and thematic development, and also the great pianist Arthur Rubenstein.

She told me about her new boyfriend, who was studying to become a botanist. She was serious about her work as a pianist and she was a solid A student. She was taking driving lessons, buying new clothes, changing her hair and nail styles. She was moving into adulthood, and I knew she would leave home someday too.

One night we were getting ready for bed. Manon had slipped out of the shower and toweled dry, and we both began to brush our teeth over the porcelain sink.

"Mom," she said, "are you going away again? Are you going back to the jungle?"

"Yes, darling. I'm afraid I really have no choice."

"But you're better now. Why do you need to go?"

"I'm exploring something," I tried to explain. "But believe me, I would never do anything that would make me stop loving you with all my heart. No matter where I go, I will always be your mother. You are so exquisite. I can't believe you are my own flesh and blood. One day, when you want to, I'll take you to the jungle so that you can experience the raw beauty in South America. We will go together."

She looked at me with searching eyes, then scrunched up her face. "But, Mom, I want to stay in places that have bathrooms and mirrors, and I don't want to swim in the rivers to bathe. You know how terrified I am of bugs and snakes. I don't know if I want to go. I might not like it."

Manon was in a phase of taking excruciatingly long showers, putting on matching underwear, applying perfume, wearing lipstick and eye makeup, and doing her hair with care. Three years after this bedtime chat she would accompany me to Ecuador, befriend a baby ocelot, swim in the Pacific, cover her eyes during the daredevil bus rides along the rim of the Andes, canoe the Napo River with natives, and walk through the rainforest with me. But for now, she needed mirrors and steamy showers in tiled bathrooms.

As August came to an end, I packed Manon's things for school: sheets, towels, clothes, lamps, rugs, lotions, shampoos, Band-Aids, lozenges, aspirin, and numerous items she needed to live on campus. There was much to do. And I was preparing for my own departure.

"Honey, I'll be traveling back and forth from home to South America. I'll be e-mailing you every chance I get when I'm in Ecuador and visiting you at school when I'm in New York. We'll see each other here at home, too, almost as much as if I never left."

Even with all the talk, I could see she was bereft. She held it in, though, and it broke my heart. I knew my leaving was like the threat of drought and famine to her. She saw that I was drawn to a faraway world, one that did not include her. And although we did not talk about this, she knew that Miles and I were having problems in our marriage.

Both Miles and Manon were disturbed by my choice to return to Ecuador, but there was no vestige left in me that was looking for validation or approval. As crazy as it seemed, I was choosing to move away from comfort and safety. The hardships of the jungle seemed small in comparison to the new feeling that was gathering force in my life. I had *choice*! But I was ready to give up neither my studies with Carlos nor my daughter and my longtime, albeit now estranged husband, Miles.

Manon could sense what was brewing, although at the time, none of us really knew what was coming. I did come back from Ecuador in a month as I'd promised. But I was soon gone again, and for the next year I was gone most of the time.

CHAPTER FOURTEEN

Bare Arms Touching

Carlos greeted me with open arms. It was wonderful to see him again. Given the changes I'd been going through at home, seeing Carlos softened me inside, relaxing my uneasy concerns about returning to Ecuador. We went straight from the airport to one of the main bus stations. He was taking me to his homeland, where he had grown up, the place he hoped one day to build his hospital.

It was early in the morning when we boarded the first of several buses that would take us to Morona Santiago, a jungle province in southern Ecuador. During the journey, we crossed mountain passes and went through the cities of Ambato and Riobamba. The ride was as harrowing as the trip to Puyo, only longer. We had one ten-minute stop in a nondescript town to have lunch and to use the bathroom.

After eleven hours we reached Cuenca, a colonial town with cobblestone streets, wrought-iron balconies, and flower-filled plazas. We took rooms for six dollars each in a hotel near the bus station, stashed our bags, and went to eat.

"We'll be staying with my family," said Carlos while we ate. "You'll be seeing my place of birth, and I hope you will be able to meet my mother."

I didn't have many questions. I trusted Carlos's decision to bring me to his homeland. But I did want to know what he hoped for us to accomplish during my stay. I also wondered how primitive the conditions might be, but I did not ask him.

"Margarita," he said, "word has gone out here, and soon will go out in Gualaquiza, which is our next destination, that we will be performing ceremonies. I want you with me to show the people that ayahuasca is your preferred form of treatment, and I want you at my side so that you will continue developing the skills you learned in Puyo."

The next morning we walked to the Plaza Civico, the town's main market area. Men and women wore panama or black hats with their hair in long single braids. They carried burlap sacks or children bundled on their backs. The market consisted largely of indigenous women who had come from the countryside, many of them in bright skirts. They sat behind gunnysacks of beans, fresh chickpeas, lentils, potatoes, and corn kernels of various shapes and colors. We bought supplies to carry into the jungle: thirty-pound sacks of grains and rice, tarps, a chain saw (which I had brought from New York at Carlos's request, packed in a crate with a special form from Customs), kitchenware, gasoline, and motor oil. We had to make several trips to the bus. I stayed with the stuff as Carlos gave a bundle to the driver to attach to the top of the bus, then came back to get another load, bundle by bundle, until everything we had purchased was deftly strapped to the top of the bus. At about ten the next morning, we set out on the next leg of our journey.

Late in the afternoon we arrived in Gualaquiza. It had a laidback feeling with its quaint, colonial-style church, multitude of trees, and cobbled streets. It was an attractive little town, but there was nothing much to do. I didn't see the kind of commerce I had seen in Cuenca. Carlos told me that Gualaquiza had a history of colonists who came to cultivate the Amazon land for cattle grazing, as well as prospectors who had gold-mining concessions on the Bomboiza River. The colonists and the Shuar panned for gold and hunted in the forested hills for toucans, jaguars, and snakes.

Carlos's home community of Santa Marta was in the mountainous region called *La Cordillera del Condor* in the Upper Amazon basin. His home was on the border of Peru, in the Canton of Gualaquiza, near the Bomboiza River.

The wet, mountainous, heavily forested sanctuary had isolated the Shuar culture and preserved them from the westernization that was brought by the Spanish conquistadores more than four hundred years earlier. Until recently, the Shuar had led a nomadic existence that left few archaeological traces in the hot, wet climate. Pottery shards had been found in the area and the surrounding lowlands that archaeologists dated back to as early as 2000 BC. Carlos claimed that the Shuar were the original people of the Upper Amazon, and that his traditions went back thousands of years.

In the 1920s the Silesian Catholics persuaded the Ecuadorian government to set aside lands in Morona Santiago and Gualaquiza to establish a mission and to control the conflicts that had developed between the Shuar and the settlers. Still, the contact with missionaries and oil developers, and colonial expansion, had drastically impacted the Shuar's traditional way of life and continued to cause friction. By the 1950s, the Shuar had lost a considerable amount of land to settlers. They abandoned their semi-nomadic life and began to form family settlements. Nowadays, shotguns, rubber boots, machetes, and hard liquor—aguardiente—are ubiquitous in an area that not so long ago was largely untouched in its remoter parts.

Carlos and I had planned to leave Gualaquiza for his family's land the following day, but that night he had a dream that we were in danger. He absolutely refused to budge until he had another dream telling him it was okay for us to travel.

"I have seen that some men who have power are jealous that I am traveling with a white woman," he said. "They will use their dark magic and throw *tsentsak* at me, try to wrestle my power away from me, and then kill us."

"What are tsentsak?"

"Tsentsak are part of the arsenal of the uwishin or the *yachak*, a Quechua shaman," he replied. "They are magic darts that live inside the body of an uwishin. They are powerful weapons that can be used to cure or even kill. I do not fear malefic shamans, but there is no reason to call attention to ourselves. It is better not to have to fight them. As long as my dreams guide me, we will be safe."

We waited for two days before Carlos got the message we could travel. In the meantime, we occupied ourselves visiting *parientes* (distant relatives) of Carlos's in their homes.

We boarded another bus just as dawn was breaking. People were jammed together inside and hanging off the sides. Women held babies wrapped in shawls and burlap sacks filled with dried corn. Farmers carried roosters in sacks or piglets strapped under their arms. I was hoisted up the side of the bus by a strong-armed man. Carlos and I had to sit up top in the blazing sun for a good part of the morning. I clutched a metal stud on the roof as the bus, decrepit and fuming, swung down dusty rutted roads.

I baked in the sun until finally, after hours and hours of bumping, fuming, wending, and winding, Carlos shouted and the bus stopped. The driver climbed up onto the roof and began flinging bags onto the ground with ominous creaks and crashes. Our valuables rained down. We jumped from the bus to claim them. We seemed to have been let off in the middle of nowhere. Dragging everything we had, pile by pile, we came sooner than I expected to Roquafuerte, a dingy town of battered clapboard houses and muddy roads. There were no cars. People meandered through the dusty pueblo. There was a small *mercado* that sold canned food, coffee, cigarettes, and sodas, and a few houses on either side of a dirt road. Heads poked out from behind doors.

"Don Carlos!" Small dark men stopped what they were doing to greet us, whether it was chatting up a neighbor or rolling a wheelbarrow filled with plantains. Our arrival sparked commotion and excitement. Cousins, school chums, and friends of Carlos's father, who had been a respected Shuar warrior and uwishin, gathered around.

"I need some of you to help us carry these supplies to my *finca*," Carlos said. His finca, he had told me, was a farm where he and his extended family owned hundreds of hectares in the jungle.

Men seized bags, packs, and the chain saw and trudged off with brisk determination. We followed. I carried my backpack, which Carlos had crammed with tin plates, pots, and drinking glasses that we had picked up in Cuenca. I had filled it sparingly (not liking to carry extra baggage) with a towel, a roll of biodegradable toilet paper, tampons, a bar of soap for myself and my clothes, natural toothpaste, flashlights, a Spanish dictionary, my journal, portable recording equipment, two changes of lightweight clothes, my passport, and cash. I also carried a sleeping bag; a medical kit with insect repellent, antibiotics, malaria pills for emergency use, Band-Aids, and steroid cream for bites; a water-purifying system; sunscreen; two romance novels (yeah, the kind where the pirate steals the girl and takes her to the Caribbean), and, of course, lipstick.

"Americana? From Los Estados Unidos?" people asked, gawking at me. Conversation switched back and forth from Shuar to Spanish. "Who is the white woman?" people asked Carlos. "What is she doing here?"

"Natem has called her to service," Carlos replied. "Margarita knows that our traditions have inestimable value, not only for our people but for those in her world in North America. She is a guerrera"—a warrior—"and my apprentice."

As we walked, Carlos questioned the villagers for local news—family, births, and deaths. One of the men turned to me and asked in Spanish, "How old are you? Are you married?"

"In the United States," I replied, "it is not considered proper to ask a woman her age."

At first, I thought the men were rude and brusque. But I soon came to realize that they were just extremely curious. In Ecuador it is terrible for a woman to be divorced or single. She has to be attached to a man to be a part of the society.

Then came the stunner. "We see you walking around with this black man here in our town. Why do you do this? Doesn't this bother you to be seen with a person who has skin his color?"

Carlos waited for my reply. The men looked at me in earnest. They didn't seem to be prying; they were just confused.

"Black. White. Colors needed for a checkerboard," I said. I placed my forearm next to Carlos's. We all stared at the two bare arms touching. "I think the colors look good together," I said. "Skin tone makes no difference to me."

The men were as dark as Carlos. They looked astonished at my response. My presence in the village with him ran counter to centuries of exploitation and degradation of the native culture by outsiders. The people found it hard to believe that I wanted to be with them, learn from them, work with them on their own terms, rather than convert or change them. I was a rarity; I wouldn't see another white person during all the trips I made to this area of southern Ecuador.

CHAPTER FIFTEEN

Madre

The conversation continued as Carlos and the men and I strolled out of the village, leaving behind the sounds of Roquafuerte and its petite civilization. We trudged on and on into a wall of steamy forest. We were pestered by biting flies and no-see-ums—small, maddening mosquitoes. The heat was stifling and I was carrying a heavy weight. But I was back in the jungle, and I felt like kissing the ground. I said to myself, this is *el oriente, la selva*. My pores opened and my body sang: "Yes! You've brought me to the right place. This is where I belong!" It was as if every joint was greased; I felt young, fluid, rich with energy. I had found my spot and it was like no other.

After we had walked twenty minutes, the ground became soggy and spongy. Mud reached to our knees, so deep in one area that water gushed down inside my knee-high rubber boots. Slippery logs had been laid for bridges over particularly wet areas. We passed a man on horseback; the animal's belly was caked in mud. Carlos told me that the land was fertile because we were in a floodplain of soil rich with volcanic deposits.

After an hour of this difficult walking, Carlos turned me in another direction and led me into the foliage, away from the men, who went on with our heavy packages. We crossed a stream and walked into the forest for about fifteen minutes. Then the forest opened and we came out on the sandy bank of the river.

"Come," Carlos said. He waded out to a sandbar.

I followed and stood on the sandy island with him.

"Margarita, stay here. I'll be right back."

I waited, but Carlos didn't return. The sandbar was desolate and without shade. I took small forays, crossing low areas of the river to see if I could see something or someone, always returning to the sandy knoll where my backpack sat. Hours passed. I was dehydrated and my bare feet sweated and slid inside my rubber boots. I pulled out an Atkins bar and ate it. I smoked cigarettes to kill time. I had a water-filtering kit to use on the river water, but the purification process to wipe out bacteria and make it suitable for drinking took hours.

I was fuming when Carlos finally arrived.

"Let's go. I've got everything organized," he said.

"Jesus, Carlos. I wondered if you were ever coming back."

"Margarita, come. I had to find a bed for you and some mosquito netting," he said. I didn't know until later that Carlos had had to prepare the village because his community had never had contact with a white person.

We pounded through the shallow waters to the river's edge and made our way north on a footpath until we came to a small meadow. A few buildings made of clapboard, palm thatch, and cement enclosed the area. Beyond the tiny village was the endless mosquito-ridden jungle.

The closest home was Carlos's. I entered and dropped my pack. I met Nube, Carlos's wife and the mother of his first nine children. She had two young ones in tow, the offspring of another man. Nube was petite and the color of light mahogany, probably about my age.

Her hair was cut just below the ears, black and shiny. She looked strong and capable, and she was dressed in shorts and a T-shirt—Western clothing. She was barefoot. I liked her immediately.

The house was built with open windows, palm trunk supports, and a thatched palm roof. The room was sparse. I looked at the makeshift bed with mosquito netting. It was oddly plopped down in the room.

"Carlos is going to have to fix that today if you are going to sleep there," said Nube, pointing. I looked up. There were holes in the roof over the bed. I knew that the torrential rains that were part of jungle life would soak me. I suspected Nube might not want me there, but Carlos hadn't given her a choice.

The room was about twenty by thirty feet, furnished with a roughly hewn wooden table and three chairs made from local mahogany. A propane tank for cooking sat on a wooden platform against a wall. A machete lay on the floor—it was the only kitchen utensil—and next to it was a bucket. A hammock was strung in the middle of the room where Carlos would sleep. Nube showed me a room tacked onto the main room where she slept with her children on a low pallet made of wood and bamboo. She kept a few private things in there—clothes, of which there were not many, for her and the children. A brown-and-white dog scuttled by.

Nube and Carlos went at it in Shuar, about what I had no idea. She was feisty, reacted sharply, and then appeared downcast and apologetic. Carlos intimidated her, I saw, and like a doe she backed up, cowering as he raised his voice. I didn't like the implication that she had to obey him, nor did I know what would happen to her if she didn't.

"Woman, make food now!" he shouted in Spanish. She jumped as if he would beat her and began cutting plantains off a giant five-foot stalk with the machete. Her eyes widened as Carlos brought in the supplies from Cuenca. She looked at the food ravenously. Later I would learn that Nube had been cutting down trees on the land, selling them for a few dollars. Carlos had been livid that she was destroying the land for short-term gain. But I could see that she desperately needed money. Carlos told me that he supported her as much as he could.

Their relationship was complex.

Carlos had lived with Nube and their nine children until the war between Ecuador and Peru broke out in 1995. He'd been conscripted into an elite unit of soldiers because the Ecuadorian government considered the Shuar "violent savages" and fierce warriors who were capable of outlasting the enemy in the rough, mountainous jungle terrain. While he was warring, Nube had taken a lover. Upon Carlos's return, they fought. Carlos took his children—including Mauro, Nube's oldest son—and moved out. Nube's young ones by the other man stayed with her. Although this was Carlos's home, Nube was still the mother of his children and this was where she stayed. I would later find out that Carlos had "homes" with various cousins, uncles, and aunts all over Ecuador, as he did in Puyo, in places like Sucua, Macas, and Quito.

"Your house is so simple and efficient," I said to Carlos.

"We Shuar prefer open spaces, in nature and in our homes," he replied. "We are proud of our modest existence. We keep only what is essential. Our food is plucked from the earth and cooked. We need nothing saved or stored. We live day to day as we have always done."

"Where I come from, our homes are crammed with things."

"We could never live that way because everything must be moved to a different area of the house at least once a month."

"Why's that? It seems like so much work," I said.

"To keep the energy always moving and fresh. This keeps families healthy and happy," said Carlos.

Nube swept the concrete floor while the plantains boiled. The house had been built about thirty feet from the Saka Entsa River. I peeked out of the back window and saw young girls bent over boulders, scrubbing clothes at the water's edge.

It grew dark quickly. Nube turned on an overhead lightbulb that was run by a generator. She put the infants to bed; then she grabbed the dog that had been traipsing about. Carlos propped its mouth open with a stick, then poured a copious amount of ayahuasca down the dog's throat. Nube had complained that the animal was sick, so Carlos was doctoring it. Soon it began howling and running around in circles until it was raving and wild, whimpering until it found its way outside. That was the extent of the doctoring. When the dog was finally corralled after great effort, we got ready for bed. I quickly removed my pants and lay down under the mosquito netting in my T-shirt. The dog whined and moaned, but my need for sleep overtook me.

The next morning the dog was bounding up and down as if nothing had happened to it. "We Shuar always have dogs," said Carlos. "At night we keep them tied to the bed that we and our children sleep in, because they are guardians and protectors. They are precious to us and our women will give them breast milk should the pups be motherless."

Suddenly, Carlos got up from the table as if on cue and I followed him outside. In the distance, I saw a woman coming out of the jungle. She was barefoot in a blue dress. She had a tiny plastic purse with her that was flattened and empty. Her black hair, which fell to her waist, was parted down the middle and grew so low on her forehead that it looked like she was wearing a fur cap. As she came closer, I saw that her face was leathery from age and painted with achiote. She was thin, dark, and powerful. Her face was open and non-judgmental. Carlos knelt down at her feet with reverence. I saw her spindly brown legs.

"Margarita," Carlos said, "this is my mother, Maria Juana."

She was Aguarana, one of the members of the tribes of the Jivaro (meaning "wild and rude," a name given to the Shuar by the Spaniards, which the Shuar loathed). The other "Jivaro" tribes were the Shuar, Achuar, Huambisa, and Shiviar. Tales of the Shuar's warlike demeanor and fierce unwillingness to be subservient had given them a mythic reputation in all of Latin America, along with their eerie technique of head shrinking, known as *tsantsa*. In the 1970s the Ecuadorian government made it a crime to kill a man to take tsantsa.

Maria Juana had come from her home in the forest where she lived alone. At eighty years old, Carlos said, she was still cutting palm daily to survive. Maria Juana spoke to Carlos in Shuar. He translated: "I dreamed a woman would come from a land far from here. This woman who stands before us is whom I dreamed. She is my daughter. I have been looking to all my female children for the one I can pass my powers to when I go to the next world." Carlos was one of the youngest of nine children. "My children here are not ready. This is my daughter whom I have been waiting for. Tell her I have dreamed this."

She brought my head close to hers and whispered in my ear as Carlos translated. "When I die I will pass my powers on to you. The tobacco smoke will rise and my power will flow into you."

"I am honored, my mother," I replied and kissed her on both cheeks. We held each other tightly. I felt overwhelmed by her pronouncement and I turned her words over in my mind.

The three of us made our way to the house. Carlos's family members began pouring in. I had no idea where they came from. His sisters arrived: Cici with her kids, Mariela, and Chavela, with three children who stood behind her, watching. Two of his brothers, Angel and Manuel, also appeared. They exchanged warm embraces with Maria Juana and Carlos. I noticed how fit and handsome the men and women were. Everyone seemed both curious and shy in my presence. Manuel said, "We have never seen a white in our community. You are the first."

Maria Juana bent down to pick up a pot on the floor. She walked over to me with the vessel in her hands and motioned for me to drink the clotted liquid. I took a sip and passed the bowl back to her, but she insisted that I take more. All eyes were glued on us. I drank again of the milky substance, which tasted like rancid cottage cheese. She motioned again, and I finished the bowl. I had taken too much, I realized. The substance in the bowl was alcoholic, and I felt a little drunk.

I came to learn that it was *chicha*, always offered first to a guest in a ritual of welcome. Maria Juana had made this batch herself days before, starting by masticating yucca in her mouth, then spitting into the pot, where the saliva and yucca fermented in river water. The longer the fermentation, the stronger the potion. Individual saliva—always a woman's—had different tastes and Maria Juana was famous for the distinct taste of her flavor that brought satisfaction to the men's lips.

Even though chicha is the Shuar's daily drink, like water is to us, it is always served for ritual purposes. Usually, the highest-ranking male drinks first, followed by other men in the community. In the acceptance ceremony, the visitor is offered chicha again and again as a sign of respect, but the guest is expected to decline after the first taste. I was embarrassed that I had drunk the bowl in its entirety. Still, after I had emptied it, the refilled bowl was passed around the room several times and each family member drank. I giggled, tipsy, and sipped as it passed me.

When the acceptance ceremony was over, Carlos sat next to his mother and put his head in her lap. He began to cry. He fawned over Maria Juana and told her how much he loved her, how much he had missed her. More relatives came into the house and soon the room was crowded and noisy. Everyone was speaking in Shuar and I couldn't understand a word. There were children and infants underfoot, plus a few stray chickens, and the wiry brown dog whipped its tail through the crowd. People talked loudly and pressed into one another. A radio played somewhere.

I walked outside and others followed. Cici had an infant strapped on her front and she held the hand of twelve-year-old

Carmelita, her daughter. Carmelita had big wet expressive doe eyes outlined with thick black lashes.

"Carlos said that you have come to live with us. Are you *really* from the United States?" Cici asked. She was beautiful, with long hair tied back from her face and puffed up at the crown. Her eyes were Egyptian under dark full brows, and her perfect lips curled delicately. She wore a sleeveless white blouse with worn oversized reddish pants and sloppy rubber boots. She might have been thirty or thirty-five years old. I met her eyes, imploring me to reveal something that I could not discern. Her nostrils flared, which I took as a sign of strength and control.

"Yes, I am from a place called New York," I said. "It is far, far away from here and it is a part of the United States."

Then she asked how old I was. Was I married? Was I Carlos's wife? Was I rich?

"So many questions," I said. "I hope we can share many things together."

Cici looked at my clothes—khaki pants and a tan hunting vest whose bulging pockets held my tape recorder, glasses, cigarettes (hidden from Carlos), bug spray, a canteen of water, and a disposable camera. I pulled out the camera and asked Cici to take a photo of everyone. She was delighted.

We all lined up and she snapped a shot. I took portraits of her, Carmelita, Maria Juana, and Carlos. Then Cici snapped photos, posing people in different groups.

"Carmelita is a shy girl, but she wants to know if she can touch your hair," said Cici.

"Yes, of course, if she allows me to touch hers too." This seemed to delight everyone, and we all began to pat one another's heads. I thought of the contrast of my pale skin against theirs; my curly blond hair was so different from their long ebony silk. They were somewhat afraid of me but also in awe.

"*Rubia,*" they said. Blonde.

About eight children followed me inside the house. They were curious, touching me, pulling on me, laughing. I went to my pack and pulled out dinosaur tattoos I had brought from New York. I asked Carmelita to get me a bucket of water and we all marched outside again. I sat down with the kids and pasted an animal on my arm. They lined up for their own temporary tattoos. Maria Juana appeared and asked me to place a T rex and a brontosaurus on her forearm. She was very proud of them and would not wash them off in the coming days. Soon we were all tattooed. I had seen the crude real tattoos on Carlos's thighs, inked when he was a soldier. One leg had an eagle, the other a jaguar.

Carlos's family maintained their language and lived according to age-old customs, imbibing the ceremonial chicha and eating a traditional diet of yucca, plantain, peanuts, *chonta* (a species of palm nut), poultry, and beef. Most of the family and their neighbors grew plantains and *Naranjilla* (a citrus fruit), cut chonta palm, and sold yucca—the main sources of cash for buying household goods. A few more wealthy landowners in the area raised cows for export and sold timber.

"We Shuar have kept much of our ancestral culture, cere-monies, and values," said Carlos. "We are bonded in solidarity and communal work. We are a proud warrior tribe that has never been conquered."

The Shuar believe that in each family is an anciano (an elder) or a *varón* (male child) of great power. This person interprets dreams and counsels the group. Carlos was *kakaram*, a warrior of valor, who, through initiations, had confronted the terrible spirits and wrenched their power away from them. His dreams, like Maria Juana's, were "seeing" dreams, full of prophecy and portent. So even though Carlos was younger than some of his brothers, he was the designated elder who advised his family in all marital and prop-erty issues.

His connection to higher, numinous power was the most important criterion for this choice: Social power was connected to spiritual power. It was here in the bosom of his family that I finally saw Carlos most fully in his element, most completely himself. His personal charisma and power—built on simplicity and the beauty of his people and their ancient traditions—was reflected in the faces of his family. He'd earned the right to be their leader.

CHAPTER SIXTEEN

A Billowing Light

The next morning, Carlos brought me into the village proper. About twenty lean-tos and huts were huddled together, a short distance from Carlos's house across the meadow. A long wooden structure, the local primary school, reminded me of an ROTC building. It could have housed more than forty pupils, but that morning it was empty.

Carlos walked me through the village. "You are going to meet my neighbors," he said. But the neighbors, it seemed, didn't want to meet me. Doors slammed shut as Carlos and I approached.

"Come. Come outside," Carlos said. I was utterly unprepared for the shock on the women's faces. "Do not be afraid. She is a good friend and my apprentice."

"Carlos, leave them be. I don't want to cause any grief at my presence."

Carlos grabbed hold of a middle-aged woman. She pulled to get back into the house and wouldn't look at me; she straddled the doorway as if she would run inside if things didn't go well. Carlos's smile just broadened. His black eyes glittered in the bright sun. He squeezed her lovingly, enchanting and mesmerizing her, winning her over.

We went through the village, knocking on doors one by one. The ladies of the houses dared not defy Carlos, and they all stepped outside. He smiled, coaxed, and charmed each and every woman. *Boy,* I thought, *they really love him.* Shyly, they'd peek up and take a look at me. After a few such meetings, the tension eased.

Near the river, a few men watched our progress through the village. Mickey was about five foot three and thin, with wide Amerindian cheekbones. He wore army fatigues, a green baseball cap, and the ever-present *gomas* (rubber boots), and he held the chain saw I had brought from New York.

"Fire it up, Mickey," Carlos said. Wood chips sheared into the air as Mickey buzzed through an already felled mahogany tree. Carlos watched in satisfaction and then took the machine in hand; his arms began shimmying as he cut the broad trunk into six-inch sections. Mickey would make tables from the planks. Manuel and his two wives came to watch. Other men, dirtied from cutting palm, and women who had previously hidden themselves appeared. I was particularly taken with Mercedes. She was clothed in a dress with a floral design that looked like it might have come from the Salvation Army; it was stretched tight across her very pregnant belly. Her hair, mussed but tied back, pulled on the edges of her wide face. The next day Carlos would deliver her baby, his two hundredth, he would tell me. Mercedes smiled at me and so did one of Manuel's wives.

We all walked back across the meadow and packed into Carlos's house once again—the new folks, Maria Juana, Nube, Cici and her kids. Everybody shouted in Shuar. Plantains steamed on the table. The kids, with their hungry eyes, were told to go outside; they were not going to get to eat. I would later learn that the children were served leftovers after the adults ate. I went to my pack and pulled out a pound of figs and handed them to Carmelita.

"Share these with all the kids," I said. The bag was devoured in minutes as the adults looked on with envy. Carlos's people were hungry. They were always trying to harvest more plantains and yucca so that they would have something to sell to middlemen who would take the produce to Cuenca for dollars. The rivers were nearly fished out, and the birds and animals once hunted for food were scarce. I could see that hunger was a permanent condition. Carmelita came and sat on my lap, playing with my hands.

Someone decided that I should record messages on my tape recorder from the people in Santa Marta to my people in the United States.

Maria Juana gathered herself in front of the microphone, stately, cool, and collected. Her people, gathered around the table, regarded her in awed silence. Maria Juana's presence was solid, like that of a great mountain. Speaking in Shuar, she invoked Uwinsut, Etsa, Arutam, Mayai, Nunqui, Takia, Shakim, and other spirit beings.

She prayed for me, saying, "We are grateful for your presence. You are here in our time of desolation. You are here to give us hope. We pray to God Uwinsut that there will be a rebirth of our ancient knowledge, pride in our heritage, and acceptance of our traditional values. We pray that our Mother Nunqui, the animals of the forest, the fish in the rivers, and the birds in the sky will return. We pray that our holy knowledge will not die with our elders. I have seen in the visions that you have come to help the Indian people and to rescue our traditional medicine practices from extinction. We are to share our knowledge with you."

She sang to me in the voice of one very young. Her singsong was a spellbinding nursery rhyme about us playing together as children in the forest. "My people are lost. They are suffering. How can we live in a different way? Pure and holy? We must fight for the truth and for our traditions. We are grateful to you, Margarita, for coming."

Others took their turn to pray, welcome me, send effusive greetings to the United States, and plead for an exchange between our two peoples. They begged for relief: money, food, jobs, clothing. When the recordings were done, Angel asked me to get a visa for him and his family to emigrate to America. A few others, who were in great need, added requests of their own. We sat together, and some of us cried. Then it was time for everyone to go. Carmelita and the children wanted to stay, but the adults knew that our moment of companionship was complete. Maria Juana stood up and everyone quickly departed.

The house was suddenly quiet. Nube and I sat down to relax while her babies played on the floor. But Carlos was revved up; he was vigorously strong in body and he seemed to have triple the energy of anyone I had ever met. He shot up a palm trunk, clinging to the wall like a tomcat. He leaned precariously high on a beam to mend the roof over my bed. Nube and I groaned at his dangerously unstable position, but he casually flew from post to post twenty feet above us with the agility of a monkey, yelling for us to climb up and hand him thatch.

Suddenly, the door burst open and Cici ran in with her six-month-old in a shawl sling and Carmelita in tow. Carlos swung down from the ceiling and Cici held out her infant to him. The boy's head was bruised and lopsided.

"I fell, I fell," Cici wailed. "I slipped on the rocks. Just before town. Juank flew from my shawl and landed on his head. Is he going to die? Oh, my God, Carlos, you must save him."

Carlos took the child in his arms and looked him over. He was like a dead weight. He handed the baby back to Cici and turned to me. "Margarita, let's get things ready," he said. We unwrapped some of Carlos's *herramientos* (healing tools) and moved the table into the center of the room. Carlos took the infant from Cici and laid him on the table. The baby was impassive and unresponsive, and his head looked grotesquely deformed. I feared that he had suffered brain damage, a hemorrhage, and that he might die.

Now it was almost six and the sky turned instantly black. Nube put Carmelita with the two infants.

"We're going to work on Juank," Carlos said to Cici. "Don't worry. Sit over there." He pointed and she sat down in the corner, her tear-streaked face buried in her hands. Carlos shut the door and cleared the room of negative energy with prayer and incense.

I stood by him as he whistled softly. Then he began singing the tune. *Be-be-be-be. Be-be-be-be.* The tones traveled in thirds, fifths, and octaves up and down the scale, becoming ever more sonorous and deep.

"No ayahuasca tonight," he said. "We will use tobacco. Fill my pipe." As I did so, he continued singing over the baby.

I stuffed the pipe, the common wooden European kind, with a dark brown tobacco that was rough-cut and cured. It had come from Carlos's pouch, and I thought it must be native jungle tobacco.

I handed Carlos the lit pipe. He sucked on it and blew clouds of smoke over the top of Juank's head. The boy howled, but Carlos held him down, unmoved by the cries. The more the tobacco poured over Juank, the more he screamed. Cici was hysterical, but Carlos would not let her come near us. The room became hazy with smoke, and the infant continued to howl.

Carlos said that he had to capture both the tobacco and its spirit for healing work. Plants, I knew, had both physical healing properties and spirits of their own. "The smoke compels negative spirits to be drawn away from Juank, and it will stimulate healing," he told me.

Though Carlos seemed sure of himself, I wondered whether it was possible for him to help the child, as badly hurt as he was. Cici really didn't have a choice. The nearest hospital was more than a day's journey away. Carlos was her only hope.

I could hear bats hissing, sounding like electronic blips and streaks in the cool night air outside, and my adrenaline spiked. I held the bawling infant in my hands as he writhed and kicked, trying to get away from the smoke. The air was dense with it.

Outside, there was a clap of thunder. Suddenly, Carlos bent down and began to suck on Juank's head. The powerful intake of his breath was noisy and loud, like a wet vacuum cleaner. Between the screams, the thunder, and the sucking sounds, the room had a chaotic urgency about it. Carlos was in a state of deep meditation or trance. He ran to the open window, where he vomited dry phlegm, then back to Juank. He repeated this action several times. When he completed the *chupando*, the sucking, he picked up the aguardiente and blew waves of the cold liquor over the child. Juank by this time was crying himself into a frenzy. I held him down with one hand and, at Carlos's command, waved the condor feather fan over him. I guessed that over an hour had passed since Cici had burst into the room.

"Margarita, hold the baby's head between your palms," he said.

I laid down the fan and I took the infant's head gently between my hands. Carlos held his feet.

I don't know how or why, but I instantly found myself in a deep trance, something that is very hard to describe. I saw two lines of light in the form of a cross. The first line traveled through the baby, a cord of light that connected me to Carlos. I realized that I was amplifying Carlos's healing energy. The second line crossed the child's chest, perpendicular to the line between Carlos and me. This line, I intuitively understood, delineated and "held" the sacred healing space that Carlos had created.

A billow of opaque light rose from Juank's swollen head. The form lifted from Juank but did not detach from him. It hovered, went inside him, and came out again. It appeared confused about whether to leave the body or not. If it left permanently, I knew that it would be a very bad thing for Juank.

The billow bounced up and down, rising like a helium balloon, sinking and lifting. It seemed to take an excruciatingly long time to decide whether to stay or go. Carlos and I held onto the child, the light line firmly secured between us. Finally, the "form" entered Juank for the last time, and I saw it meld into his body like a piece of a jigsaw puzzle locking into place.

We had been huddled over the infant for two or three hours now. Finally Juank quieted. Carlos pronounced the healing complete, thanked the Great Spirit, and told Cici to give Juank breast milk. She spent the night with us, sleeping on the floor with Juank.

The following morning, Juank was alert, bright, gurgling, and smiling. His head now looked perfectly normal.

Thinking back over the experience of the night before, I realized that I had been "seeing" without the aid of natem. Natem had been infusing me so that now I could see without it—I cannot think of a better way to express it—with another sort of knowledge. How the information arises, how it becomes a perception that one accepts and acts upon, is a mystery to me. Carlos has the simplest explanation: We have five physical and five spiritual senses, and with training, we can learn to "see" with our spiritual "eyes." I took one thing away from that healing of Juank: The training that Carlos had subjected me to had unleashed powerful, ethereal energies inside me.

CHAPTER SEVENTEEN

I Want to Be Alone

After the incident with Juank, Cici and I became friends. Maria Juana came infrequently; she was hard at work cutting palm and lived a solitary life. I missed her presence, but I hung around Nube, her kids, Cici's family, and the village children when Carlos and I were not working together.

Men were scarce in the daytime, working in the forest. I heard that several of the village's husbands were in cities in Ecuador or in Spain trying to eke out a living for their families back in the jungle. The wives stayed at home, while the young girls washed clothes by hand in the river and gathered water and wood, always with infants strapped to them. They were the workhorses of the community. They began full-time mothering of their younger siblings at the age of eight, and most girls were married when they were thirteen. School did appear to be in session some mornings, but only the varónes—boys, that is—attended. I was never introduced to the teacher.

In Ecuador, primary school is free, but families have to pay tuition for each child over eleven. The girls, I learned from talking to them, wanted to go to school too, but they had no choice in the matter. The little kings were doted on by their mothers. They never worked, but played the whole day through, and they were waited on not only by their mothers but by their sisters too. I thought this was a sorry state of affairs, so I started the Queens and Princesses Club. Any girl under the age of five was a princess; the older girls were queens.

"Us? Royalty?" the girls cried with glee. They'd never been titled anything other than worker-drones. I had never seen them play. The Queens and Princesses gathered in the evenings on my bed under the mosquito netting, giggling. The boys stood around, flummoxed, outside the veil of separation.

"You can't have a club without us," they cried. "We have to be included." I'd continued to befriend and play with the varónes, but I explained that this club was exclusive and you had to be female to belong. The girls puffed up like proud peacocks, inflaming the boys' passion to bust through the netting. Whenever they shot through I bounced them off the bed. They marched off in a huff to tell their mothers.

Meanwhile, the girls and I, all nine of us, lay together with flashlights, doing nothing much but squealing. I told them stories like Sleeping Beauty and Jack and the Beanstalk. And I began making plans to start a foundation that would pay for the girls to attend school. I thought I could raise enough money to pay their fees. But this wasn't as simple as I thought, and neither, it turned out, was our club.

I was almost continually in the presence of the children and other people from the village. It didn't take me long to realize that I felt crowded, and I began to notice that I was *never* alone. The Shuar bodies pressing against bodies, the fights, the heated discussions, the radios blaring, the infants screaming, the dogs barking— it was all nonstop. The Shuar cannot fathom anyone wanting to be alone, ever. It's not part of their culture. It was difficult to understand this tight human interaction because it was so different from the way I'd grown up. As a child I had my own bedroom and I was accustomed to doing homework and playing the piano by myself. As an adult, I'd always had private space to work, sleep, or simply be. But here, if I walked outside alone, Carlos sent someone to bring me back. At some point I realized that when Carlos was away, he was putting me—without telling me—in the charge of one of his relatives, usually a man.

One morning I woke up an utter mess and I couldn't find tampons in my backpack. This was a big problem in the jungle because I didn't know where to buy supplies. I ripped a T-shirt to use, but first I wanted to bathe and wash my pants. I decided to take a path along the riverbank—alone. I didn't tell anyone I was leaving.

Hah! I'd escaped unnoticed. *What a relief*, I thought. I hid myself behind a stand of trees at the water's edge, took off my clothes, and slipped into the water. It felt good to clean the sticky blood from my legs. I began scrubbing my pants.

Suddenly I heard voices. Nude, cranky, and PMS'd to the hilt, I turned around. Most of the village had come out to keep me company! They waded into the water with me and started making inane conversation.

"We didn't want you to feel lonely so we've brought some of our wash," said one woman.

Carmelita stood beside me in the water. Mickey was on the bank with his chain saw. Mercedes had her new baby. Then Nube and her kids appeared. I wanted to scream, "Leave me alone!" But I knew they wouldn't understand. They were being sweet and attentive. I scrubbed my clothes and walked back to the village with at least twenty people in tow.

Cici fell into step with me. "Margarita, can you adopt Carmelita and raise her in the States?"

"Can I do what?"

"Will you give Carmelita a good life, unlike the one she will have here?" Carmelita held my hand and looked up at me with her adorable eyes. For a moment I let myself fantasize about taking her to the States and how absolutely magical that would be.

"Cici, that is a beautiful dream," I said, "but I don't think it's likely. I adore her. I adore you both. I'd do anything for you. But it's impossible to get a visa from Ecuador to the United States." Immigration had a no-exceptions closed-door policy at the time. Even Ecuadoran scholars couldn't get visas to give lectures at Columbia University in New York. "And even if it were possible," I added, "you would miss her so."

Days passed and pressed into one another. Carlos and I cared for many people. I helped him treat horrendous diseases: hideous wasting sicknesses and terrible abscesses from parasitic animals that burrow under the skin, eventually working their way into the brain and killing you. Some weeks we performed rituals three or four nights in a row. On those mornings I wanted to get right to sleep because it was likely someone would show up at noon with a request. We had daytime patients too. Carlos turned on the radio to ensure that sound was around us in those early hours—whatever time it was we went to bed. I could hardly stand the incessant beat of the music as I tried to drift off to sleep. He needed constant high energy, but I was desperate for silence, something I'd had no piece of since my arrival.

One morning, after we had been up all night for a healing ritual and Carlos had fallen asleep in his hammock, I slipped outside. I was desperate. Nube and her kids would soon be up. I furtively looked around the corner of the house. No one was in sight.

I went swiftly, quietly from the house, bent over, hopping from bush to bush until I reached the river. I felt like a thief stealing time. I ducked onto a narrow footpath and ran for some distance.

Finally I was alone and it felt divine. Just the birds and insects. I walked slowly, savoring the solitude.

I'd had about twenty minutes of privacy when I found a beach. The area opened expansively and the sand below my feet was white and silky. As the foliage was sparser here, I stood and looked around me for the hidden birds who sang like sirens. I knew I could find my way back to Carlos's house anytime, so I walked farther along the river's edge. I soon became aware of a slow pull on my leg, as if I had a huge wad of gum stuck to the bottom of my boot. I picked up my leg, as if in slow motion, but it was weighted down. My foot sank an inch or two in the sand and stuck. I pulled up my leg, but the movement made me sink deeper. Then my back leg began sinking. I realized that both legs were trapped and I was sinking by perhaps an inch every ten seconds. Christ. Quicksand! What should I do? I remembered from a movie that you shouldn't thrash about; that would only cause you to sink faster.

I looked for a branch, for something to grab hold of, but I was in an open area. There was a bush to my left, but I didn't know if I could reach it. Ever so gently I stretched my arms, and I sank a little more. I couldn't reach the bush. For ten agonizing minutes with no plan, I slowly sank—to my shins, my knees, then midway up my thighs. Quicksand, I later learned, is ordinary sand so saturated with water that the resulting mushy mixture can no longer support any weight. It has the consistency of newly poured cement. Although I was barely breathing—to keep myself from descending farther—the mud was now up to my hips. I had no hope of getting free. I was really scared. I didn't call out because there was no one to answer my cry.

Without warning, the bushes rumbled. My God, a jaguar? But Carlos, Mickey, and one of his buddies jumped out of the undergrowth. They'd sneaked up on me. Carlos was doubled over with laughter. They wouldn't come near me; they just circled, hooting.

"Get me out of here!" I said.

"Don't move. You'll only sink deeper." Carlos laughed.

"I know that!"

"And what did I tell you about leaving on your own?"

"Weeeeeell…" I felt like a child who'd been naughty and had to face the consequences.

"Come on. I want to hear the words. What have I told you?"

"Not to leave."

"What? I didn't hear you. Could you speak up?"

"I'm not supposed to run off."

"Why?"

"I don't know why."

"What?"

"I'm not supposed to try to get away on my own."

"Because?"

"I could get into trouble?" My voice rose to a falsetto. Still, I wasn't going to acquiesce if I could help it.

"Are you going to try this again?"

"I guess not."

"You guess not?"

"Lift me up!"

Carlos stared and waited.

"No," I said finally. "I'm not going to leave without you or someone designated by you."

"That's better," said Carlos. "Men, pull her out."

I wasn't ashamed, and I'd already gotten past feeling relieved at their arrival. I was annoyed. Though I did understand I was not invulnerable to certain "disasters," I hated Carlos when he was preaching.

Mickey got a long branch and I grabbed hold of it. He and the other man pulled, and I was sucked out of the shifting sand. I was covered in filth, so I washed quickly in the river. Then I slogged back to Santa Marta with Carlos and his cronies, who role-played: First I was a captured prisoner; then I was a damsel in distress who had been rescued by brave warriors.

The ground had looked solid. Quicksand is like that. The jungle people knew where to walk and not to walk and they could avoid the dangerous places. After my quicksand episode, I watched and noticed that they treaded lightly, whether they were walking barefoot or not. There was always the possibility of something underfoot that could get you.

CHAPTER EIGHTEEN

Rosita

When we arrived at Nube's, I wanted to clean up and hit the bed—I'd been up all night—but that was not to be. A man named Roberto had left an urgent message. His mother, Rosita, was bed-ridden and needed medical attention. Carlos said that we would have to leave for Roquafuerte at once. I changed my clothes and ate a piece of cooked yucca, Carlos grabbed his herbs and other healing tools, and we set out on foot.

Carlos rushed ahead. "Hurry, there's no time to waste." We tromped through mud, which, for me, required great effort. The flies were vicious, and I was sweating like a demon when we finally got to the small footbridge that would take us to town.

Breathless, I broke our silence. "Carlos, is Rosita going to take the medicine?" I wondered about this because Carlos never used ayahuasca in the daytime. He had told me that the sun's heat collides antagonistically with the medicine's power. Perhaps we would be spending the night, I thought.

"No, Rosita is too weak," he replied. "If we can get her stronger, then she will drink natem." I wondered how he knew her condition without seeing her. Perhaps from Roberto's note?

Roquafuerte was about to have a jubilee, and the small town square was active. A group of young men were setting up loudspeakers for a dance that would take place that night. Music and microphones blared on and off as they tested the equipment. It looked like a big deal for the sleepy town. Kids played in the street, a man went by on a bicycle, and a few roosters ran by.

Rosita lived in a yellow two-story wooden house just off the plaza. Roberto, one of her two sons, was waiting for us outside under palm trees. We climbed up to the second floor. Carlos set his two bags full of medicines down in the hallway and we entered a tiny room where Rosita was lying in bed.

Rosita was in her mid-fifties but looked much older. She was lying on her back and had trouble seeing us—she couldn't turn her head—until we bent over her. She was so bloated that she couldn't move. I touched her massively swollen arm and leg, pressing my fingertips into her flesh, but it did not bounce back. She had hands like a victim of elephantiasis, her fingers so distended that she could not bend them. It was as if her cells had exploded toxins that flooded her body and pooled under her skin. Her lymph system didn't work, Carlos explained. She was engorged, literally floating in water, but she was also dehydrated. The smell in the room was fetid.

Carlos looked her over and checked her heart. It was not the problem. He spoke gently into her ear. "Rosita, I am making a warm drink for you. Have you eaten recently?"

"No," she said weakly. "I have taken nothing for three days. Not even water. I can't drink anything. I feel so full."

Carlos told me to stay with her while he prepared the guayusa. Rosita appeared to have lost circulation in her extremities, and her stomach was the size of a car hood. She told me she hadn't slept for a very long time because she was so uncomfortable. I sat on the floor at her bedside, speaking softly to her. But when Carlos returned with the tea, she refused to drink. I gave Roberto instructions to find drinking straws.

"Rosita," I said when he returned. "You drink a little sip from this straw. Not much. Every ten or fifteen minutes I will give the straw to you. I am going to stay with you and do everything I can to help you. Carlos is here to do the same. We want you to get well, to feel better. You know your boys are worried about you."

She drank a sip, smiled weakly at me, and then laid her head down. My bedside manner impressed her, but not as much as the fact that a woman from the United States was tending to her.

I got Rosita to drink at regular intervals, and in between I massaged her swollen legs with a light circular touch. After an hour I left it to Roberto to administer sips. Meanwhile, Carlos had gone into the jungle to get a plant to treat her. I went downstairs to inspect the large quantity of fresh plants—long fibrous shoots of pale green with hollow centers—that lay on the kitchen counter in a pile as big as a Christmas tree.

"Margarita, take the machete and chop these," said Carlos. The chopping was difficult, as the plants were exceedingly tough. Like celery, they were very salty, wet, and stringy. Soon Hector, Rosita's second son, joined us. He did what he was told and never asked questions or even spoke at all, but beat the stalks with a hammer, mashing them after they had been cut.

As Hector finished each batch, Carlos placed the pieces in the *liquidora*. The plant fiber made the blender whirr and smoke. We made ten batches. After squeezing the mixture, which was the consistency of applesauce, through a sieve, we strained it into a bucket until a thin fresh liquid was extracted. Carlos was notoriously messy in the kitchen. I'd seen his work at Nube's, though he was never cooking food! Fiber, juice, and plant particles spattered the floors, walls, and counters of Rosita's kitchen. Pots, pans, and buckets were strewn about, others were filled with freshly cooked liquid. Utensils, plates, cups, and bowls had been torn out of the cupboards. Carlos made medicine and assumed that women would clean up after him. They always did.

"Bring me a bottle," Carlos ordered.

I held an empty monster-sized cola bottle as Carlos poured the extracted liquid into it. He had had Hector find a thin rubber hose. "Give me the catheter," Carlos said. He strapped it on the neck of the bottle with string and twisted a metal fastener around the tip.

"What's that for?" I asked Carlos.

"I'm making *una regadora*," he answered—an enema bag.

"But that's not going to work," I said, horrified at the idea of getting the thing into Rosita. "It needs a way to collapse so the liquid can be forced out by gravity,"

"In the jungle we make them from animal parts and plants. This is standard. We'll have no problem. She's got to have this treatment." Now Carlos was fashioning a clamp from a piece of wire to make a release valve for the rubber hose.

We climbed the stairs to Rosita. Carlos told me that Rosita would have major explosions after the treatment. "She's got uric acid poisoning," he said. "It's coming from her eyes, ears, mouth, urine, skin— everywhere. When we perform the treatment, no children or pregnant women can be around. They could be damaged by the expulsions from her. And you must be very centered and free of deficiencies, weakness, and illness to take on such a patient as Rosita. This is a dangerous undertaking."

On the floor of Rosita's bedroom stood large buckets of guayusa. We placed the liquid for the regadora next to them. Rosita's sons helped us turn her on her side. In doing so they had a chance to change her bedding, which was soiled because she hadn't been able to get out of bed.

Rosita seemed to be compliant and trusting, and I felt her pain deep inside me. She was humiliated by the state of her body and her inability to help herself. The fragility of her life touched me to my core. Through her misery, I was invited into the compelling truth about life: The presence of death is very, very real. Rosita's suffering made me feel as if my heart was going to explode.

With the help of the two boys, we lifted Rosita. She moaned as we lowered her again onto her side. I held her hand lovingly. Carlos had her sons leave the room and shut the door. Then he inserted the contraption into Rosita's backside, but the liquid didn't want to flow. Carlos was sweating; although he looked cool, I could feel that he was stressed. He called on his highest powers to help this woman. How are doctors able to operate in the hopes that their patient may survive? Sometimes last resorts are the best that we mortals can do; God and faith are invoked at the cusp of life and death. I wanted Carlos to stop, because she seemed so miserable, but I knew that Rosita was dying from poison inside her. I didn't think there was anything else that could be done for her.

Finally, after much repositioning of the tube, Carlos got liquid into her. She cried out, he removed the tube, and she defecated into a bucket we held. Water poured out from inside her as if a dam had broken. The smell of rotting flesh filled the room. Carlos asked me to leave the two of them alone, and I moved into the hallway, where the smell of disease had spread. I waited and called upon my God to spare her life.

Then Carlos summoned me back inside and asked me to talk Rosita into another go. In her state I wondered how she could endure any treatment, but I held her hand and began praying with her. Carlos looked concerned and frustrated because the treatment she needed was weakening her, possibly to the point where he wouldn't be able to do any more treatments. Meanwhile, Rosita began to vomit. She was white as a ghost—pale and deathlike.

"Rosita, the regadora and the guayusa are going to clean out your insides and take away poisons that have built up inside you," Carlos explained. "It's also going to make a lot more water come out of you, and this will make you feel much better. Your body won't be so swollen and you'll be able to move."

Rosita's sons stood outside the door looking terrified. Carlos came out into the hall and spoke to them.

"Is she going to live?" Roberto asked.

"Yes, your mother is going to get better," Carlos said. "But it's going to take some time. She's very weak, but we can build up her system."

We'd been with Rosita since morning. It was around four in the afternoon when I stepped onto the street for a break. I was walking around Roquafuerte when I ran into Cici. I was desperate for a cigarette. Rosita's treatment was hard for me to bear and nicotine usually relaxed me. "I know where you can buy some cigarettes," Cici said. "Come, Margarita."

She took me to the market that I had seen when Carlos and I first came to town. I went to the window and bought tampons, four cigarettes, and matches. I handed two smokes to Cici and I lit up. I blew smoke rings and sighed. We walked around the park, watching the sound technicians set up, and then we stood beneath Rosita's window.

Just as I took a big drag, Carlos looked out the window. His face fell. He didn't like me to smoke, especially manufactured cigarettes, except in ceremony. "Your health," he would say, "will suffer." Now he gesticulated wildly but silently, because he didn't want to disturb Rosita. I wagged a finger at him. He couldn't stop me from smoking. I really needed those cigarettes to calm me down.

In the evening, Carlos and I left. Rosita promised to take sips of the guayusa every half hour—or at least to drink some water. She felt somewhat more comfortable and a little color had come into her face. We had turned her a few times and I had massaged her, which had physically stimulated her. She had no more treatments. Carlos had treated her as much as was possible given her lack of strength. Her skin was still puffy with edema. Carlos promised to return the following day and administer more treatments with plants.

"Rosita, you'll be able to sleep tonight," he said. She responded with a thin, sweet smile.

I begged Rosita to drink the guayusa every half hour, and then I spoke to Hector and Roberto. "Be sure your mother drinks this throughout the evening," I said. We hugged. The boys looked haggard with fear.

Outside the music was starting up in the square. People had gathered, and life went on as Rosita drifted off to sleep.

CHAPTER NINETEEN

The Women of Gualaquiza

The lights of Roquafuerte rapidly faded. We stumbled along the jungle path to Nube's in the dark, or rather I did. Carlos held my hand most of the way, and he walked steadily. Neither one of us had anything to say. I was using my feet as eyes, and I let go, trusting my tired legs and Carlos to guide and keep me upright. The light from a quarter moon helped. It was about nine at night when we arrived in Santa Marta.

When we reached Nube's, both of us were ready to drop. Carlos swung his bags inside the front door and looked up. Sitting in the middle of the room was Nube, her cousin, and three other women whom I'd never seen before. They'd come from Gualaquiza early that afternoon and had waited for our return. We'd barely gotten our bearings before they rushed over and began telling us about their ailments. It seemed the youngest of the three was in a deep depression.

I was getting used to people coming in at all hours of the day or night and expecting Carlos to treat them. I sighed because I knew we were going to conduct a ritual. Carlos never turned anyone away. He had the energy of three strong men. My energy is labile; when it's flared out, I need to recuperate.

Carlos enlisted Nube and her cousin to attend the ceremony. That made seven of us. I followed Carlos to get the natem and prepare the altar for the ladies from Gualaquiza. Carlos turned to me and said, "Margarita, prepare yourself."

I wanted to sleep, although I knew the medicine would keep me going all night, for days if necessary. With every ritual I was nervous, afraid of going insane. I could never predict what would occur, no matter how many times I took the sacred vine. But each night I drank from the cup, I would be in the presence of spirits that launched me into psychic realms of ecstasy and terror. I drank *la medicina* because of my deliberate intention to learn, and because it was my job, my path, my dharma.

I spoke of my terror to Carlos before we began the ceremony that night. His response surprised me.

"You have nothing to fear. *La medicina* never drives one crazy, nor does it kill," he said. "I have been drinking natem for over forty years, yet I want to run away every time I am called upon to conduct a healing."

That was reassuring in one way: I would not go insane. But it was not reassuring at all that after decades Carlos wanted to run away too. It really didn't matter what he said. I knew that I would drink.

Carlos consecrated the ayahuasca and offered the sacrament to each of us. We settled in. No one spoke. I waited for the effects of the medicine and considered the deeper death of the ego I would surely undergo. With *la medicina* there was always knowledge that only the ayahuasca was in control. I sat on Carlos's right. The three women from Gualaquiza, with Nube and her cousin, were arranged in front of us.

The medicine hit me hard. Carlos looked at me through the eyes of what I could only describe as a symbolic mask. He was no longer himself. He looked like a mythic archetype, an animated thing that was millennia old. He relieved me of my healing duties. Carlos's figure yelled, "Go now!"

A strange beast that I came to name the Emissary was barreling toward me at an unconscionable speed. I rushed to the far end of the room and sat in the warrior pose, waiting for something terrible to happen. The Emissary held me in His thrall. He posed on a pedestal next to me and glommed onto my spirit. I somehow knew He inhabited realms unlike those here on earth, and He spoke in whimsy, but with ominous overtones. The Emissary was incessant, insistent, and no matter what I did, He would not go away. He played jokes on me and frightened me. I felt absolute horror, and I wanted to get as far away from Him as possible. I was back on the razor's edge again. The words *It only gets worse and worse* kept running through my mind.

The Emissary's body was small and humanlike, but He had an animal head with laser-luminous eyes that looked like a cross between a fox and a tiger. He had come to me during several prior ayahuasca sessions, and when He came I knew that I was in for it. The Emissary was Guardian of the Treasures, but I always had to go through hell to get the prize.

He smiled at me like the Cheshire Cat, then grabbed hold of me. I begged for mercy, but I was spun upside down and hurled through a volcanic gate—a window to the underworld. I was sliding into hysteria. I saw many visions at a dizzying pace as I fell. I tried to scramble up the vortex, but the suction was relentless. And then suddenly a voice startled me. "Focus now!" it said.

I gathered every bit of my willpower to cull the images coming at me. *Focus now!* I grabbed onto an image as if it were the last foothold on a cliff. Focusing, or becoming "sober" under the medicine's influence, was a near-impossible task.

Once I managed to slow the images down to a blur, they abruptly stopped. The underworld's dense gravity continued sucking me down, this time toward unconsciousness. I tried to hold onto an image, any image, or bring the cascade of visions back, but my mind was like viscous tar, as if my brain survived on delta waves that had slowed down to zero pulse; it was as if I were submerged three miles under the sea, with the pressure of the whole enormous ocean on me. My awareness landed in emptiness that was black and velvety, although it was without form or color. The density was not a color. I could not see my hands or body; I was immaterial. But my inability to see my body did not defy my certainty that what I was experiencing was real. None of my senses—touch, smell, sight—were of any use here. I had no thoughts!

After a time, which felt like eons, a voice spoke to me. "You must stay conscious, aware. Do not fall asleep. You are in the place where all creation forms. If you do not remain awake, your chance for consciousness will disappear forever. Remember these words. You must understand that what you know as waking life is a form of sleepwalking. You are in the land of pre-form; although it is not a place, it sustains the world you walk upon.

"Fight to keep conscious and remember what you are experiencing now. We will continue to teach you."

I can't say how long I stayed in the place of Creation—an indefinitely long time. At times a thing or an idea would materialize from nowhere. I "saw" the beginning of things generating from nothing, no precursors to form!

Five Tibetans on horseback, dressed in vermillion cassocks, rode like the wind into the void.

"We have come to pull you out now. You've had enough. You have succeeded in your task." With those words they hoisted me up onto the back of one of the horses. We flew.

I was back. I could move and look at my body. The Emissary began His torturous tactics on me, and I was terrified that He'd send me off to another dimension again. He attached his spirit to mine and held onto me like a sadist. Now, however, I could perceive with my own senses. I had shaky control, but control nonetheless, over myself. But however hard I tried, I could not get rid of the Emissary. I just accepted His presence.

Carlos was bent over Nube, and he beckoned me to take a look at her. It was almost dawn. Nube had diamond-shaped objects inside her that I could tell weren't supposed to be there. They sucked filth into her like magnets. I could "see" hidden things within her body, not the way Carlos could see, but I knew that the power of awareness had revealed itself to me. I knew that the Emissary's dimensions contained within them powerful healing forces, if I could learn how to tap into them.

Carlos laid two large crystals on either side of Nube's pelvis. He explained that crystals healed uterine problems, because they worked like a laser that burned out sickness. But first he taught me how to know the strength of the quartz.

"To test a crystal, use your tongue to feel the energy of it. We never use our hands to do this. Try it." He showed me how. I placed the crystal so that it was barely touching the tip of my tongue, and I immediately felt a strong electrical current that traveled to the back of my palate and throughout my body. To this day I find this a simple way of selecting crystals for their energizing effects.

After about half an hour, Carlos removed the heavy quartz and had me feel Nube's stomach. She had a large cyst, near her right ovary. I touched it, managing to feel the very bottom of the tumor.

Nube screamed.

"Margarita, be careful," Carlos said. "You've got to go in slowly. Know what you're doing. You hurt Nube." He spoke to me as if I were a clumsy intern. I apologized to Nube and winced at my stupidity. My skills were rudimentary. I felt barbaric. I had hurt her. *I hurt her.* My head screamed.

I walked out of Nube's house, feeling like a dolt, but also knowing that something tremendous had occurred. That night in the black void I had traveled beyond horizons of time and space. I had gone to the place where the shaman's work is conducted. Time and space, I'd understood, were potentialities that interacted. They were building blocks of physical form. Time was where the living on Earth existed. Between the on and off pulses, the beats of time, there were infinite worlds within worlds. Without focus and consciousness, one could be obliterated between the beats. Blinked out.

Dawn was breaking. Across the field, the women from Santa Marta were going down to the river to gather water, while inside Nube's house slept the women of Gualaquiza.

CHAPTER TWENTY

God of the Black Jaguars

Carlos slept an hour or so after the ladies from Gualaquiza left, and then he went back to tend Rosita in Roquafuerte. I stayed in bed until two o'clock. Nube had slept in too, but was gone when I rose. By the time I had dressed, she had returned with wet clothes in hand. She'd been at the river washing laundry.

I walked outside and rested against the front of the house. I watched as a man on horseback carried a giant stalk of plantains, going from house to house to sell them. Nube sat next to me; she was glad to get me alone because she wanted to explain her side of the breakup with Carlos. They had been married at a young age and she had given birth to nine of his children.

"I know Carlos has told you about my affairs with other men," she said. She was small and the dampness curled her short hair around her face. Luckily the humidity in the high Amazon where Santa Marta sat was nothing compared to that in Puyo.

"He has," I replied.

Nube countered with a list of the infractions he'd committed, things I didn't want to hear. In general, Carlos left her alone, then punished her by sleeping around. I later learned he'd been inducted into the army in 1995 and was gone for two years. I assured her that I had no acrimonious thoughts about either of them. Things between a husband and wife should remain private.

Nube stood up, as if this would lend weight to her pronouncements. "I'll never share a bed with him again," she insisted.

"Well, you don't have to. Why don't you divorce him?" I said.

"He's the father of my children," she said. "Besides, when he visits he brings me food," she said.

Now Carlos was coming down the path. Both Nube and I stood to greet him. He liked that, and he teased Nube, saying that she was and always would be his wife. She frowned and spat something at him in Shuar. His face looked innocent enough, but certainly not shy. That smile of his paved the way into places most men dared not go. His charisma bordered on a guru's.

Carlos had been at Rosita's most of the day. "Rosita will not receive ayahuasca," he said. "She is dying and too weak to continue treatment. There is nothing more I can do for her." Then he slipped inside the house.

Nube had something on her mind—the real reason, I began to realize, that she'd come to sit with me. I waited as she formed her thoughts. She dawdled, but finally she came out with it.

"Margarita, would you be godmother to my youngest child, Mankash?"

I hadn't been expecting that! I knew the hardships she faced, and I understood that in her mind having me as godmother would ensure that I would always send money for food. Her kids would not grow up hungry. My heart went out to her. I realized that I was more than ready to accept the responsibility for Mankash and the bond that would tie me to Nube for the rest of our lives.

"What a sweet surprise, Nube," I said. "That would please me so. It would be an honor."

"I'll go to town and find the priest so we can set a date," she said.

"Nube, let's do a ceremony without a priest," I said. "I don't hold with the views of the Catholic Church."

"But we must have a priest! That's the only way he can be godmothered," she cried.

"I came to your homeland because of the teachings of your people and natem. This is the spirituality that I hold in my heart. I can't participate in any aspect of the Church."

Nube looked at me in consternation and began to argue. I cut her off.

"One of the reasons Carlos wants me here is because I stand up for the old traditions. The Catholics have called you devil worshipers. That is ridiculous, offensive, and just plain wrong. The sacred medicine is my spiritual path. I will be Mankash's godmother, but the Shuar ritual is the only way that I may participate in claiming him."

Carlos's family had been baptized, Christianized, and believed firmly in the Church's rituals. Nube couldn't understand my point, but I was not about to have anything to do with a Catholic priest. I never became Mankash's godmother.

Carlos came out and told Nube to prepare dinner. "Margarita, let's go sit by the river," he said to me.

We splashed water on our faces, arms, and legs and sat down on large boulders. I knew Carlos must be tired; after dinner he'd probably go to sleep. He seemed tender and spoke quietly. It was as if he wanted to confide in me, and suddenly I found myself listening with the ear of one who is intimately involved. He was letting me into his personal history, his private life.

"When my father sent me to the missionary school in Bomboiza," he told me, "I learned of Jesus. I was only twelve. I had dreams about airplanes, shoes and radios, all modern and civilized, like the white man's religion. But at school the racism was very hard to take. I couldn't speak my own language. I begged my father to let me come home, but he said that I had to learn the ways of the white man so I could be a leader for my people in the new world that was coming. I wanted to be back in the jungle, catching frogs and hunting with my father. I wanted the medicine so that I could be strong.

"Before I left home, I lived in a large *elliptico* compound that held our family and one hundred warriors. My father had two wives who each had nine children. We had a great fence for protection and four sentries watched day and night. High trees surrounded the outside walls and we used a very tall tree for our lookout. Our living quarters had an earthen floor, walls made of chonta palm, and a roof of palm leaves.

"The living quarters were separated into three areas. The area for the women and children was a restricted zone where our father would visit us. Behind the family area, beyond a separation wall, my father sat to greet visitors. Our sacred ritual items, our weapons, and poison darts were kept here. In the center of our compound, which was 100 meters [325 feet] long, there was a hole in the ground that opened into a hidden tunnel. It led far out into the land and came up near a great tree where we kept more rifles, blowguns, and spears. The third and largest part of the compound was where my father's warriors slept.

"After a few years at school I had a vision where I was taken to the world of my ancestors. Uwinsut told me to go home and take the path of the warrior. I ran away from school and went back to my compound. I'd missed my mother and family desperately. This time, my father did not turn me away. I studied with him and the other great uwishins. Since that day I have been on a path of service and love."

After telling me all this, Carlos went into the house and came back out with a photo of his father, Andre. It was a sepia print that had been eaten away by jungle fungus. I saw a solitary man leaning against chonta palm. I could hardly make out the features on the small face. Except for the title to Carlos's family land, this picture was all that was left of Andre and his warring life.

"My father knew that our lifestyle, customs, and identities were being degraded. He said to me, 'When I first came to this land with my wives and two children, the forest was virginal. I claimed the land. We had fish and meat to hunt. My wives planted the gardens and bore many children. Then other relatives began to come here. I led our families and we grew strong.

"'During this time your uncle was a great, great medicine man. He was so revered that a Quechua tribe whom we were at war with asked that he come to heal their leader, who was very sick. I gave permission for him to travel with four guardians. The Quechua promised his safe return.'

"My uncle was a beautiful man with long, silky black hair and facial decorations that made women swoon. They all wanted to be his wife. He was going to bring back many riches from our enemy in exchange for curing their chief. But there were enemy warriors who did not know about the exchange, and they slaughtered my uncle and his guardians as they traveled through the forest. When my uncle's body was brought home, the women tore at their hair, wailing. My father went into a rage and killed ten times more Quechua men than the Quechua had killed of ours. War went on for months and months. My father took the head from each dead man and made tsantsas.

"But while my father was fighting our enemies, the Spanish came to take our lands. My mother organized the women. Well hidden in the trees, they murdered many soldiers and colonists with blowguns, and never was one of our women killed in the battle. Finally, the Spanish turned away in fear, knowing they could not win a battle with an enemy they could not see. Little did they know that the person who led the slaughter was none other than *mi madre,* Maria Juana.

"My father died of old age. More colonists and Spanish came and stole the tsantsas and sacred objects from my family. The heirlooms and holy pieces were sold for great sums of money, none of which our family saw. Our enemies' heads now lie in museums in Spain, Cuba—all over the world. I know each of the dead men's names. Their shrunken heads sit behind glass in museums for all people to see.

"My father's vision of the new world had come true. Our traditions are dying out. I am one of the last uwishins left."

I learned from Maria Juana that Carlos's Shuar name, given him by his father, meant God of the Black Jaguars. Maria Juana said that when he was born, the shamans knew he was going to be a healer and his father took him to a sacred island where his first taste, even before breast milk, was ayahuasca.

"My mother's father was known as Maestro Juank," Carlos said, "because he was one of the best-known ancianos of the Shuar people—a priest, a doctor, and a medicine man. He was one of my great teachers."

I heard stories of Carlos's family and of his own training as a shaman—his rigorous process of initiation. He told me about one initiation ritual at a waterfall. "I had to be alone to guard my purity," he said. "No woman could touch me or send me greetings. I had to build a fire for myself alone in the night. I prayed to the *Gran Espiritu* of the *cascada* so that Tsunqui, the spirit of the waters, might bless the plants that I used in healing. I drank the natem, ayahuasca. I vomited and had a rectal bath. I drank bowls of tobacco water, praying nude and fasting for days. Only then was I able to cleanse myself in the waters and be purified.

"After some days, I walked toward the waterfall, touching every stone on the path. I sang, and then I screamed and slapped the rocks to let the spirit of the water know it was time to wake up. The wakes and whirlpools in the waterfall rose up; *las aguas* flung waves into the air. The wind rose and blew in every direction. I found a sacred healing stone that had been spit up from the waters. All the time, I prayed for purification.

"I called on the maestro of tobacco. I called all the vengeful spirits, the spirits of all the dead, the spirits of jealousy and hate. I invited them to come to me, and the soldiers of the ancient spirit of tobacco captured them. I bottled these spirits in a hole in a rock, pressing down with more rocks to cover them. They would be judged and justice handed down by the Gran Espiritu.

"Finally, I was invited into the waters. Fish lived there in sacred places; their houses were very cold. They knew all the secrets of the abyss. The fish lived together with the ancianos, guardians of the fountain of life. I was purified and received *Arutam*—power, God force.

"Later, I put on my clothes and returned home, but for days I stayed in purity. I held it in my body for as long as I could."

I listened to Carlos's tales in a kind of reverie. I loved hearing them. I had shared moments of my own past with him, my own private fears; I understood that he trusted me. And I was starting to think that his feelings for me were deepening. I realized I wanted that.

CHAPTER TWENTY-ONE

A Crystal Palace

After an early dinner, Carlos finally slept. Nube tended her children quietly. I wrote in my journal and took advantage of much-needed rest. That night, the rain on the roof sounded like a battery of soldiers marching overhead.

When we got up in the morning, the river had risen right to the back of the house. The rivers and tributaries are notorious for flooding their banks, going from peaceful waterways to swollen torrents when the curtains of water come down. We were practically in a lake.

Around noon, the sun came out, the air steamed, and Carlos and I went to the dry side of the house to pound ayahuasca vines for more medicine. Carlos kindled a fire. When it was burning well, Maria Juana arrived from her jungle home and sat down with us. She had a burlap sack with her. A giant black and red rooster flew out of the bag with a great squawk. It showed me its behind and shat right in front of me on the ground. It flapped its wings as Maria Juana handed it over to me. She said something to Carlos I didn't understand.

"She wants you to have this token of her affection," said Carlos. She'd offered me the equivalent of a twenty-four-karat-gold bracelet in our culture. She didn't eat meat herself; it was too costly. Stunned, I wanted to return the bird to her, because I knew she couldn't afford such an extravagance. But instead, I thanked her profusely.

The rooster was so angry and hard to hold on to that I put it inside the house and closed the door. Maria Juana sat quietly. *My God*, I thought, *I love this woman dearly*. Her soul was open, innocent, and she was transparent, like a rinpoche—a clear, unaffected soul and an example of goodness. Although we could not converse—she didn't know any language other than Shuar—her strong presence spoke for her.

After some hours sitting together while Carlos and I tended the ayahuasca, she went into the house to visit Nube. When Carlos and I were alone, he grabbed my arm. "I am frightened," he said, watching my expression closely, "because tonight the ceremony will be terrifying. I do not want to do the ritual, but I must."

"Why, Carlos?" I stammered. "Is something bad going to happen? And why must you do it?"

Carlos looked at me with his eyes full of fear. He would not, or could not, answer my questions.

"Cancel the ceremony," I said. "Please, Carlos. You're frightening me."

He stared at the ground, his elbows resting on his knees, absorbed in a profound meditation. "The ritual must continue as planned," he said eventually. "I can do nothing about this. But you must prepare yourself. And don't tell *anyone* what I have told you. *Not one word*."

The hair rose along my skin as Carlos stood over the kettle of medicine, cooking the ayahuasca down to a thick mixture.

"Remember the protections I have taught you," he said. "You will need them tonight."

That evening, with Maria Juana, Cici, and Nube, we walked to Manuel's hut, a structure of rough wood slats with some straw strewn on the dirt floor. Manuel and his two wives, Carlos's older brother Vicente and his wife, an elderly man, and two children were among those waiting for us. They huddled together tightly. As darkness fell, I looked around, nervously remembering Carlos's prediction. Everyone waited with reverence and acceptance. Their respect for Carlos was deep and their belief was pure, holy.

Carlos looked ominous, with warlike symbols, diamonds, and wavy lines painted all over his face and forehead. His prayers were solemn and fierce. He asked me to bring a vat of medicine and place it in front of him. As I held it, he sang into it, infusing it with power. His utterances strengthened and protected the medicine, and they contained the force and spirit of his guides. I peered inside the ayahuasca and felt as if I were falling into a deep bottomless pool. When he was finished singing in the spirits, Carlos gathered his power in the base of his belly. Like the blast of a fighter jet shooting beyond the sound barrier, his breath erupted from him with a rushing vibration that shot through the room on the winds of a hurricane. Carlos was a force of nature.

I sat back down quietly, afraid. We had all taken medicine. Carlos had taken three times the amount that I'd seen him drink before.

When the medicine hit, I flew out through ever-widening spirals. Carlos's tumank undulated and buzzed. I was aware that people were dropping on the ground like it was Jonestown all over again. I observed from a great height that the fallen could not be resuscitated. I thought that Maria Juana might be dead. This horrified me, but suddenly I had to let go of the thought. My limbs became heavy and my head nodded onto my chest. I did everything in my power to "sober" myself, but it was very difficult.

I grabbed a pillar and hoisted myself to the standing position of a warrior with bow and arrow. I was frightened about my difficulty in controlling myself physically. It was like being underwater, confused, not knowing which way was up. With great intention, I willed my body to move at my command while still allowing the visions to proceed. I stepped outside the hut and sucked in grounding energy, then staggered to the bushes, absorbing their vibrations. I filled myself with the energy of the earth and the stars. I shat, braced myself with the vigor I'd received, then returned to Manuel's hut.

Carlos was staggering and acting strange. There was no one behind the mask of his face. He appeared unaware of his surroundings and of me. I knew that something was terribly wrong.

Carlos fell down and did not move. I shook him, but he did not respond.

I cried out, wondering what to do. There were several people around, but no one could help me help Carlos. Everyone was immobile. I grabbed Carlos's condor feather and began to fan him desperately, sweeping it over his body. I put all my might into the action and prayed loudly. He didn't move. I fanned harder and yelled at him, "Carlos, I command you to wake up."

I held Carlos in my arms, calling his name again and again. After an interminable time, his eyes finally connected with mine. He choked and gasped for breath. He seemed not to know where he was. He choked again, as if he were starved for air. I took the aguardiente and blew it into his face. While he caught his breath, I looked inside his flesh. His organs were pink and healthy.

"*Ayudame*," he said. Help me.

"You're doing fine," I said, grateful that he was conscious. I grabbed his arms and legs and smacked them with my hands and the condor feather. I put my arms around his chest and squeezed him.

"Can you talk?" I asked.

"*Sí. Sí.* You saved my life. I was dying. I wanted to die. Margarita, I looked from afar at my body. I saw my decrepit flesh and then looked upon my radiant spirit that was watching me lying on the floor. I moved away from my body and up into the heavens. It is so beautiful there; there is a crystal palace with mansions and rooms that contain seductive, beneficial powers and knowledge. They entice you with peace and love. I saw my spirit helpers, great beings of light; I saw violet, turquoise, and carnelian light radiating, shimmering with immense love. My father stood at the rising stairway to take me away." His eyes locked on mine. "You have lassoed my spirit and brought it back here. The condor feathers have the power to call a person back into their body. You have saved me from certain death."

I believed he was right. Was this what he had dreaded when he told me how afraid he was of conducting the ceremony? Carlos the uwishin should have been able to dodge something like this, but this time he hadn't.

He grabbed me and held me tightly. I felt like I had done something very right. Then he looked around the hut and stood up, completely in control of himself. He took out a container full of odious liquid—a mixture of tobacco juice, powerful herbs, and aguardiente. Whenever he had had me drink it before, it had always made me vomit. This time, he told me to snort it up my nose. I tilted my head back and poured liquid from a small glass into one nostril.

"Snort it up high, Margarita," Carlos said. It felt as if a bomb exploded in the middle of my brain. Things went blank—no thoughts—and then mucus poured out. Carlos made me snort again through the other nostril. Then I ran outside and vomited on the ground. I needed the cleansing for what was to come.

"Margarita, let's get my mother," said Carlos. "She is very sick."

Maria Juana was limp. She let out a small cry as we lifted her and carried her to a blanket on the earth floor next to the fire. Carlos brushed the hair from her forehead, and then we removed her blouse. She was thin, with strapping muscles. Her old, wrinkled skin clung tightly to her body.

Carlos sang gently to her as he searched her flesh with his hands and psychic eyes. Her ancient body needed to be pumped with life force; there were energy blockages from head to toe. Carlos told me she had lumbar problems, arthritis, bile in her system, low energy, and a constant headache.

Suddenly Carlos was not the loving son, but the consummate healer with a patient under his charge. I thought he was unduly harsh, although I could see that my emotions were probably coloring my observations. I wanted Maria Juana to feel comfort; instead, it seemed all she felt was pain. She was difficult to work on, begging Carlos to stop his massaging of the joints and tendons on her arms, shoulders, and chest. She screamed and vomited. I wondered that this warrior woman could become so childlike under Carlos's care. I knew that she was unused to this treatment; with Carlos's long absences and no other uwishins in the area, his family had not been attending natem ceremonies regularly for years.

Carlos sang louder and continued his work, letting me know that I was to follow Maria Juana's head with a bucket whenever she needed to throw up. Finally, she stopped retching. As he continued working on her upper body, he asked me to stimulate her hips, thighs, legs, and feet. I began hesitantly. She seemed to be in so much pain. But Carlos yelled at me to "get in there" and move the energy.

"Don't be so timid! Use this." He handed me a ball of jet-black volcanic glass and demonstrated what I was to look for and how to use it. I could feel spots under Maria Juana's skin that I knew shouldn't be there. These I loosened with the obsidian, moving it in a counterclockwise motion. Later, when I asked Carlos how it worked, he replied that it pulled negative energy out of the body.

"I use my fingertips in the same way that I showed you how to use the ball," he said. "My elders, the people of the Aguarana tribe who live in Peru, taught me the use of enemas and many other ways to heal. They have used stones to open blockages in the body for centuries. When the negative energy has dissipated, I pray to

Arutam to bring the energy through me so that I may charge the sick person with life energy. I use my hand in a clockwise spiraling motion and the healing energy flows in."

All the painful pressure Carlos had applied during my healings, I now learned he called *diji punctura*. It appeared to be similar to acupuncture. After he stopped the fanatic pressure, I could feel energy, blood, and good things move into the area where his fingers had been. It seemed to be a kind of surgery without cutting into the flesh. I empathized with Maria Juana now because I knew how painful it was.

I finally reached her feet, sometimes using my hands, sometimes the obsidian. She was moaning faintly. Carlos fanned her with the condor feathers, which were elaborately encased with red string wound around a long handle. Maria Juana groaned, stunned and exhausted.

Carlos took tobacco and burned it over the fire. He crumbled the leaves and stuffed it into the pipe that he always used for ceremonies. "Ritual smoke-blowing bestows a blessing or protection against enemies, both visible and invisible," he said.

He blew smoke over Maria Juana, then passed the pipe to me. I smoked it and handed the pipe to Manuel. Others who were conscious took puffs too. Tobacco made the ayahuasca stronger and the visions more concrete. Its effect was something like pitocin, which is sometimes given during childbirth. It spiked quickly, amplifying sensations and contractions. The tobacco was also an offering and a request for the medicine to be as potent and visionary as it could be.

After I smoked, I reeled. Several dark spirits were with us in the room. This was normal when working with spirits, but it was always scary. Souls, both good and bad, are passing by humans all the time. One tries not to attract the bad ones, for they *will* come!

Carlos replenished the pipe and breathed smoke into the top of Maria Juana's head. Outside, the night sounds rose ominously. My skin felt alive, itchy, as if something were crawling on me. Smoke from the fire seeped through the cracks in the hut's walls. All the family members were stretched out quietly; the children who had drunk the ayahuasca were sound asleep.

"Give her a *baño*," Carlos ordered, startling me.

We took Maria Juana outside. The sky was clear and filled with bright moonlight. Bushes hedged the area, haloed in light, quivering as if they were alive. The density of the jungle, three hundred feet away, was like a black smear on the landscape. Maria Juana was whimpering. Carlos sighed; it was his mother, after all, and he did have tender feelings for her.

Maria Juana stood like a drunken person, shivering, and began to weep. Carlos nodded for me to begin. I picked up the half-gallon container of aguardiente and took liquid into my mouth in big gulps. It tasted of cheap perfume, alcohol, and gravelly, coarse sticks and herbs. The liquid puckered the inside of my mouth and made the flesh of the insides of my cheeks, my tongue, and even my gums swell.

I dare not fail, I thought. With great force, I sprayed the liquid through my teeth. It came out mixed with my saliva in a blast of fine mist. I covered Maria Juana with the mixture, spitting all over her head, back, face, chest, and arms.

When I finished, Carlos and I walked her to the garbage pails of guayusa to clean her stomach. She begged me not to make her drink the medicine—to plead with Carlos on her behalf.

"*Bebe!*" Carlos shouted. "Drink!" She swallowed, quaked, and Carlos tilted her head down to vomit. Carlos told me to keep making her drink, and then he left to go inside the hut.

After making her drink and puke again and again, I helped Maria Juana get dressed. She was shivering; her blouse was sticking to her skin from the bath of aguardiente I had given her. We sat on the ground for half an hour as I warmed her in my arms. Then together we went inside.

CHAPTER TWENTY-TWO

Union

Without warning, Carlos spoke fiercely to me, pointing at Manuel. "Heal him, his wives, and his children." Then he left the hut.

Was he joking? I waited, but he did not return. I flew into a panic. This was the first time Carlos had left me alone with a patient. And he hadn't given me instructions or even told me what was wrong.

But I had to try. I picked up the shiri-shiri leaves and rattled them over Manuel. I had just begun to sing when Carlos returned. He watched me, his arms crossed over his chest.

"Cure him," he said, and left again.

Manuel was stiff and unresponsive. I didn't really want to touch his body. When I did, he complained, "You're tickling me." I felt completely out of my depth. All my fears came up. I knew that Carlos wanted to see if I could do this alone, if I was ready. He was always testing me and this was one more test. He never let me rest.

I knew that this test was to strengthen my belief that I could do healing work. It took so much faith and conviction to do the work for which I was being trained, but I lacked confidence in myself. Then another thought crossed my mind. Perhaps I was making too much of this. Both Carlos and I were so tired. Maybe he just didn't want to do the healing himself.

I started singing again as I worked on Manuel. I was still very nervous. Touching him was extremely intimate. I did what I had been doing all along with Carlos: massage, tobacco smoke, and energy transmission through my breath.

While I worked on Manuel, I had fantastic visions. I saw brightly colored, cartoonlike lizard creatures jumping at me. Biting monkeys flew around the room. Dead souls came, and vampires. The creatures were terrifying. I had to duck down whenever one buzzed by.

My interior eyes were fogged with fright, and looking through them was difficult. Whenever Manuel groaned, he brought an angry energy that flowed straight into me. I flinched, rubbed heat into my hands, and sat on my haunches, gathering the force to move the stuff out of me and into the air above us. I used the rattle, which "ate" the negative "sparks" that came from Manuel's body.

He and his wives, whom I worked on separately, were docile and trusting. I was afraid I would hurt them, especially Manuel's infant daughter. I was afraid I would miss something. Singing, touching, and moving around them and on them, I prayed for faith.

The family did not have any serious illness that I could detect. They had the usual stresses, muscular, skeletal, and spiritual, that came with a life of hard work and poor nutrition. When I was through, I felt that I had helped them. Their ailments, it seemed to me, were mostly emotional or psychological. I was able to infuse them with the cleansing energy of love.

When I finished that night, I was physically wasted. Used up. Tired beyond words. Daylight was shining through the rafters. Roosters crowed, their heads sticking through the palm thatch, watching me. It was still dark inside; only the embers of the fire burned. People were sleeping huddled together, peacefully. I stood up, left the hut, and went to the guayusa and drank. I vomited several times, and then I turned, shivering from the chill in the early-morning air.

Carlos returned, looked around, and seemed pleased with the work I had done. He told me to spray the aguardiente mixture on Manuel and his family. I said simply, "No, you do it." He did, then closed the ceremony.

As we left for Nube's, Carlos asked me, "Did you enjoy the ceremony?"

"When I'm healing people or participating in ceremonies, I feel completely fulfilled, in my rightful place in the world," I said. "If I continue to do these things and allow the ecstasy to unfold, I believe my health will be maintained."

"You are right," said Carlos.

I had had three days and three nights of no sleep. I was light-headed, floating. I had hypnogogic visions as I walked down to the river and splashed water on my face. I lay down to rest on the sandy beach before moving back toward the house. *I'll just lie here for a minute*, I thought.

I was surprised to find that Carlos had followed me. He lay down next to me. Suddenly, my mind was whirling. It was as if I were a child, all wound up after missing her nap. I desperately needed rest. Why was I so agitated?

"I can't sleep!" I told Carlos. I felt like crying.

He lay close to me. He saw how strained I was and he began breathing into my ear—low, soothing, constant. "I am the black jaguar," he whispered. "My breath, the jaguar rhythm of my panting, will merge with your vibration. I will captivate you with the rhythm of the jaguar, and you will be able to sleep." He was in jaguar form and manly form at once. He moved his body against mine. I pushed him away again and again. I didn't want this. He had his family. I had mine.

All the time he kept up the jaguar breath, taking in and blowing out air in a soothing and constant rhythm. The cadence captured me completely. I felt as if the *viento*, the wind, was all around us, the throbbing of life renewing itself. It calmed me and I sank into its warm caress.

"Let me feel your spirit," Carlos said, "and our energies will intermingle comfortingly and with love." And I surrendered to him.

Our sexual union was extremely powerful. The act was natural, unaffected. I had not felt that kind of touch or tenderness in a long time. Afterward, I fell asleep in his arms.

Carlos had once told me that as a jaguar he could do anything that jaguars did. "This includes their walking," he said, "and also their leaping, panting, and coughing." He told me that he could put a special medicine in the jaguar tracks that he makes in the ground; the medicine would make a woman follow him. Sometimes he performed this service for men who required it.

He didn't need to bewitch me in order to seduce me: We were deeply bonded. I was completely absorbed and fully engaged in the adventure with him: the healing work, the lurking danger, the ecstatic visionary journeys, the dizzying exchange of knowledge between teacher and student. To say that he was like no man I had ever met would be a vast understatement. I had been his patient, I had been his apprentice, and now I was his lover.

CHAPTER TWENTY-THREE

Bird Bones and Plastic Bags

We heard from locals that Rosita had died. I was startled because I thought Carlos had told her sons that she would live.

"Did you know she would die?" I asked him.

"I knew, but I wanted to do everything I could for her, at the very least, help her to feel more comfortable. She *could* have lived longer."

"But why did you tell the sons she would definitely live?"

"It would have done them no good to know she would die. Rosita wanted them to have hope."

"Did *she* think she would die?"

"She wanted to live."

"But doesn't lying only make it worse when death comes?" I asked.

"No," he said. He looked sad and tired. "It makes no difference whatsoever."

I felt overwhelmed by her death, painfully aware that tending very sick people is difficult and depressing work. I suddenly felt that I had spent the last six months up to my elbows in blood, mucus, feces, and decay. Our souls may be divine but the flesh rots.

Carlos had treated people for thirty-five years. He wasn't God. He couldn't cure everyone. People died. I was looking squarely at the great suffering we human beings endure. Tending Rosita had awakened a deep compassion within me, and I felt as though I had lost someone of my own flesh and blood.

"We are all the same body, the same soul, and the same being," Carlos said to me when I told him what I was feeling. "We are both divine and corruptible flesh."

Still, with all the hardships and pain, I thought that life as a healer was luminous, inspiring, and heroic. Healing is the holiest work—and it comes from a deep, humbling place inside the heart.

The day after Rosita died, Carlos called me outside to help him pick up plastic bags. We dug through dirt and under leaves to clear the land of debris. "Do you realize that plastic bags have polycarbons that take three hundred years to break down before the earth can absorb them?" he said.

After four hours of being bent over, my hands covered in mud, we had a good-size pile of discarded plastic bags. Carlos was trying to decide where the refuse would be disposed of, when Mauro appeared.

"Papi!" he cried. They embraced, and then Mauro gave me a loving squeeze. He had been in Quito, in charge of Carlos's family while Carlos was away. He had traveled two days, and he was pleased to be home with Nube, his mother, whom he hadn't seen in over a year. He disappeared into the house to surprise her.

At eighteen, Mauro was sophisticated in some ways, while in others he was just a kid. I felt that my presence in the Amazon had changed his perspective. He had begun to see more clearly the potential of what Carlos was doing beyond the villages and poverty and limited scope of the jungle. But he and his father were different; I could tell that he was struggling to be his own man.

Carlos had gathered the villagers together to talk to them about the plastic bags and about taking care of their environment. "You take your things out, throw the bag onto the ground, and trample it into the earth," he said. "This is destroying the land. One day your food won't be able to grow here."

Littering the land seemed to be indicative of the sense of hopelessness the Shuar felt. Apathy, resentment, and despair had colored the community. Alcoholism was rampant, and many of the men had left their wives and the jungle to find work in the cities. Carlos wanted to help his people regain their respect for themselves and for nature.

As his father was speaking, Mauro arrived in the village center with Nube on his arm. "It is sad how helpless my people have become," he said to me. "Our community should never have abandoned our customs. Our elders had the culture, language, and *artisania*—artistry for bowls, clothes, jewelry, music-making, dance— and it's getting lost.

"By the time I was born, things had changed. Friends I went to school with were ashamed to speak our language. I had dreams of learning more of the white man's knowledge—to learn how to read and write and study how modern people think. I forgot how to value myself during that time. Young people my age want televisions, radios, and tennis shoes. They are ashamed of our uwishins. They say that we are maestros of the devil.

"Knowledge of the sacred medicine is disappearing. But natem is a powerful healer. I have *mucho respeto* for it and I will give myself to it so its wisdom won't be lost. As long as I am alive, I will continue practicing the sacred rituals."

I asked Mauro if there was a profession he was interested in pursuing in addition to his path as an uwishin. "I want to be an astronaut when I grow up," he earnestly replied. "I want to take off in a rocket ship from Cape Canaveral and fly above the earth."

I had a good idea how much had changed. I'd seen old photos of the Shuar's daily activities: dancing and fishing; elders in ceremonial dress wearing crowns of feathers and long, feathered earrings; women in knee-length blue tunics with thick hip belts of seeds, waist and shoulder bands made of bird bone, and necklaces made of jaguar teeth; and the hand-woven striped ankle-length skirts the male elders wore. Dress, economy, and way of life all expressed the dignity and naturalness of the people.

I had come into the Shuar community in search of wisdom and knowledge that I felt my culture sorely lacked. This in turn helped Carlos rekindle interest among the Shuar in their ancient practices and values. He met with several members of the community to talk about reviving their artisan traditions—making necklaces, weaving, building furniture from the local trees—as well as renewing their religious and ceremonial work. He organized groups for traditional singing and dancing.

"One day our lives will be enriched through the selling of our crafts," he said. "The continuation of our true way of life will reinvigorate our inherent pride and respect for our culture." Then he announced that a ceremony would take place at the *Isla Sagrada* (sacred island) the following evening and that everyone was welcome to attend. "Please tell everyone that they may come," he said as he closed the meeting. "Tell them to bring the sick. Natem will heal them."

An elder named Jose approached Carlos. "If the white woman from the United States believes in our traditions and that our medicines can cure, we will come to your ceremonies. It is good that you will lead us, Carlos, in the sacred ritual once again."

After the village caucus, though, Mickey pulled me aside. "The elders are upset with you," he said. "You can't tell the girls that they can go to school. If you raise money for their education, I'm afraid that you will be killed. You can't impose your views on us of how our society should work. The men are very angry at your ideas and words."

I was taken aback, but Mickey was dead serious. This caused me great distress. I'd so wanted to help Carmelita and the others.

In Shuar society, a woman was the property of a man. Men were t[
hunters and held ultimate authority in the family. Women work[
the fields, knew herbal remedies, and had babies. Young fema[
were the laborers that made life in the jungle possible. Th[
couldn't get out of their life of servitude and they knew it. [
education. No jobs. No hope.

I took Mickey's words seriously. I knew that although [
abhorred the role that women played in Shuar society, I had to [
go of my dream of sending the girls to school. Life was hard [
Morona Santiago. I would later learn that within a year, Ci[
Chavela, Maria Juana, and others left their homes to look for wc[
in other parts of Ecuador.

Mickey also told me that Carlos and I were in danger. Otl[
shamans, it seemed, were jealous that Carlos was traveling with[
white woman. Plots were afoot to kill us, and we had to watch c[
backs. How much of this was real? I wondered. It was hard to te[
Feuds went back generations between Carlos's family and otl[
families in this remote outback. Murder, by all accounts, was[
common occurrence. I had heard of several while I had been [
Santa Marta.

"Working in the jungle is dangerous for me," Carlos sa[
"Other shamans have tried to break through my armaments." The[
armaments were invisible; they were weapons that covered [
body, including knives, spears, darts, and the equivalent of canno[
that not only shot out ammunition, but encased and protect[
Carlos and his powers.

I asked Carlos about what Mickey had told me, and [
concurred. I was not to bring up women's issues in Santa Ma[
anymore if I valued my life.

CHAPTER TWENTY-FOUR

Possession

Most of Carlos's people had turned their backs on ayahuasca healing, but they would be with us at the ceremony at the Isla Sagrada. Carlos and I, with a few locals—Cici, Carmelita, and Juank, who was doing just fine after his injury—left in early afternoon, walking single file in rhythmic monotony through primordial swamps and dense clusters of mosquitoes, and up steep bluffs. We were encumbered by all the equipment we carried, the deep thick mud, and the dense heat.

We had walked for almost two hours when we came upon a small lean-to, open on both ends, hidden in the dense foliage. The structure was lopsided and looked as if it was about to collapse. The forest around was dank and desolate.

When we entered the lean-to, I was surprised to find Maria Juana inside. She was silent, perhaps absorbed in meditation. She sat on a log in front of a raging fire made from two ten-foot branches. She nodded at a bench, a thick log reserved for visitors. This was her home.

It was smoky and bare, except for a small bamboo bed with a

cover and one blackened pot in which herbal tea boiled over the fire. Light passed through the walls and thatch above. I'd given her a beige cashmere shawl for the cool nights, but I had noticed that Cici had been using it to carry Juank. Maria Juana's empty plastic purse lay on the bed. Nothing else was in sight. Where was her food?

She passed around a bowl of tea. A chicken strutted by a post that held up the sagging roof. Maria Juana's movements were deft and simple. She was regal, commanding, and not inclined to share her thoughts, which I was sure could only be profound. I looked into her eyes and she seemed to drink in the contents of my mind. Carlos and Cici bantered with her in Shuar. Then we stood up and took our leave from the Queen of the Forest. She considered me Carlos's wife and was planning to acknowledge me at the Isla Sagrada.

Carlos and I headed down a steep slope of mud, weeds, coca plants, and high grass. Bamboo thickets and palms spread over the land. We came to a spit of beach dotted with massive rocks. The river was raging and crystalline, interlaced with dead branches and boulders the size of cars. I dipped my hand into the water; it was ice cold. Across the river, the mountainous wall of jungle soared, a vertical mass. We stood on the secluded beach, which had been used for ceremonies by countless generations of Shuar, admiring the towering sacred island.

I spread myself over a boulder near the water's edge and let the sun invade me. The beach was like a moonscape. The rocks held cuplike pits, gargantuan fallout from once-active volcanoes, I thought. The land and water had a pureness and a desolation.

As I lay on the boulder, Carlos bent down, gave me a kiss, and sat on his haunches. "In my father's time, my people would drink ayahuasca from these holes," Carlos said. "From out of the rocks." I felt as if I could lie there forever. This wilderness was paradise.

I took off my shoes, stuck my feet into the white sand, and watched as the Shuar began gathering at the river. The women had blankets, pails, and children in tow. The men began setting up areas for their families. Women beat fiercely with stones and shovels at something in the sand. I saw that they were crushing black crustacean-like bugs the size of Ping-Pong balls that were lying just under the surface.

"Very dangerous," one of the women said to me. "You get bitten by one of these and you will feel a fire like none other. These *animalitos* are painful."

This was a paradise with bugs. I quickly put my shoes back on and got to work setting up the altar and cooking fire with Carlos. We kept at it until late afternoon. When the ayahuasca was almost finished, Maria Juana arrived, along with Mauro and Nube, who had brought drums and Carlos's violin. Mauro was wearing a big-faced watch and a T-shirt that said *I Love the USA*. He got to work fetching water and tree limbs for the fire.

After Carlos and I finished preparations, I took a walk along the beach. I hadn't been gone long when dusk fell, agitating the animals and birds of the forest. Shrills and screams arced overhead. I was wandering between the boulders far from the fire when Mauro caught up with me. "Give me your flashlight," he said. "I'll be right back. And watch out for snakes!"

After twenty minutes, he hadn't returned. It was pitch black and impossible to navigate through the boulders without getting seriously hurt. I needed my flashlight! I waited and waited. The sounds above the tree canopy were frightening. Bushes rustled and my skin crawled. I could see the fire at the other end of the beach and the shapes of people moving around. I called out, but no one seemed to hear me.

Finally, Mauro came back from the jungle. I grabbed the light and rushed toward the group, stumbling wildly over the slick boulders that were jumbled together like car crash pile-ups. I slid in right next to Carlos as he was about to begin the ritual.

Some thirty-five Shuar were gathered, sitting on blankets.

Maria Juana sat on Carlos's left side and I sat on his right. Mauro was farther down the beach with his mother and her kids; I wouldn't see him until the next morning.

Carlos introduced me to the group, invoked the spirits of the Isla Sagrada and then shared natural tobacco with everyone. A man who I later learned was Cici's husband played an old hand drum with a rhythmic persistence that blended in with the rising and falling insect sounds. Maria Juana sang, her voice a series of animal cries, human cries, and primal ululations. The fire crackled and snapped. I remembered what Carlos had said about sacred songs. "When I am singing my expressions and words are not my own. These are the words and songs of the cosmos and Great Spirit. Music is of divine origin, passed down to uwishins from generation to generation. The spirits brought the music to earth." He spoke of the magic potency of music and the skill of those who could transmit the "secret."

Maria Juana was communing with the spirit world, transmitting secrets. She carried the knowledge of natem in her blood. Her voice was like an aural illusion that melded with the natural sounds of the forest and the rushing water. Her voice was the forest. My body felt very centered as she turned to sing a sacred song naming me wife and daughter. The river sparkled in the bright half moon, and the constellations stretched overhead; Orion was particularly bright. A red moth alighted on a great stone beside me, reaching with its long antennae, which began to spin slowly counterclockwise in sync with Maria Juana's singing. We hadn't even imbibed the sacred natem. She is a powerful wizard, I thought.

The people of the forests of Bomboiza sat silently with a matter-of-fact demeanor, bathed in an aura of perfect simplicity. When Maria Juana finished, Carlos looked around the assembly, nodded that all was well, then prayed. His people came to drink from the cup he held to their lips.

Once they were seated, Carlos played his violin. His silhouette was set off by the fire and dissolved in a mist emanating from the forest. Carlos the uwishin, the wise man, the medicine man, had won his people's trust. He rode with them back into their history, back into their sacred practices, into the great source of wisdom and understanding that they had developed over thousands of years. He took them to a timeless place where the distance from their ancestors was negligible. I saw how his people responded, relaxing into him. They were fascinated by the mystical aspect of the rite, tuning into the blood heritage of their own ancient ritual.

Carlos began the healings. I sat with Maria Juana, who had curled into her own dream. I looked around; everyone was lying down but Maria Juana and me. I heard retching from the dark bodies strewn about. By this time I was engrossed in my own developing sensibility. There was a whirlwind of sound and an electric current that flamed over my skin. Visions roared as I was drawn into the realm of a powerful spirit.

The air of unpredictability was given coherence by Carlos's powerful control over the session. He managed the otherworldly currents, a task that required great endurance, willful intent, and the grace of the spirit doctors. Carlos worked on a man who'd been laid out on a blanket ten feet away from us. He called to me and handed me the shiri-shiri.

He was bent over Cici's husband, Raphael, who was screaming, vomiting, and bleeding from the mouth. Blood oozed onto the sand. Cici looked at Carlos in horror. I was to fan Raphael with as much energy as I could.

Raphael groaned and brought a dark energy down into me. I recoiled, dispelled the black tar from my body, then sat in the warrior pose and continued to fan him. The leaves blew the *mal aires*—bad air, or spirits—from Raphael's body. They shuddered with the wind, rattling a dry chorus in harmony with the rushing river waters. The fan swirled and the air became full of invisible spirits. Carlos broke out in a penetrating chant.

Instantly, an entity entered my body. An Amerindian warrior who wore archaic regalia possessed me. This was different from any experience I'd had before. This entity had purpose and was using me for something extraordinary. With his supernatural force, the Amerindian turned my body into a conduit for his healing powers. The flowing energy he imparted went through me and into Raphael.

Part of me stood on the sand watching as Carlos worked on Raphael's chest; another part of me looked on from a distant place. My arm swayed furiously. When I looked down, I saw the arm and hand of the Amerindian.

The warrior had taken possession of my organs, blood, bones, and brain. He was inside me, inside my body. The possession had come so suddenly that I was unable to follow it with my mind, but my body responded to the thing within me. His face was split down the center, one half painted red and the other black. He had the ability to look at ordinary reality on the one hand and, on the other, at what shamans call "non-ordinary reality." I, too, had this ability, because he was inside me. I knew that he was about four hundred years old and had been a medicine man when he was alive.

Suddenly, I was in a hovel with twenty or so Indians who were sitting in a circle. I had been transported to another time, another dimension. Another fire burned bright, and in front of it an old woman was laid out on a blanket on the ground, the first wife of the chief, who the medicine man told me was dying. Her breathing was very faint. The Amerindian took my body and told me that I would heal her, that this was the reason that I had been brought into the past. As I put my hands over her body and blew life over her, I was not myself, but the Amerindian. He gave me the motions, the magical passes to make with my hands and body, and the way to a cure.

This medicine man that was me was powerfully muscular and well over six feet tall. His hair fell over my ears and heavily onto my chest. He wore animal skins. His dress was unlike any I had ever seen. His hand—my hand—held a rattle made from a seeded gourd that shivered and swayed over my patient. The air whistled in explosions. The people hunched up in blankets, watching me in silence.

I rattled in a growing frenzy over the woman, my arm stiff with agitation. Eons passed. Then the medicine man within me looked at the chief. A smile broke over my patient's face. The chief and the elders rose and touched my hands, and then the chief spoke: "You have cured my wife and for this we are forever grateful. Go now, back to where you have come from."

But, inexplicably, while this four-hundred-year-old ceremony was happening—at the very same time—the Amerindian within me was shaking the leaf rattle over Raphael. I/he broke out in a grunting chant. My body convulsed. The spasm came from somewhere deep within me, radiating violently through my extremities. It was an earthquake inside me. I was shivering and muttering rapidly, crescendo and decrescendo waveforms of some unknown speech.

Some spark inside me was observing my arms and body, moving, groping. *Shuuuu! Shuuuu!* This sound rose like a siren inside me. My lungs and throat and mouth opened and it shot forth from the depths of my being, but it was not of my own making. I felt two excitements, my own and that of another, someone acting through me. I was both excited and curious; my emotions and perceptions were exulted; my mind was very far away...or was it somewhere deeply embedded in my belly? What was taking place was more urgent than anything I had ever felt before.

I heard the cries of the forest funneled into visceral chanting. Carlos was singing. He'd been shielded from my sight until this moment. He delved deeper into Raphael, finishing up the healing. I was mesmerized by the sovereignty and power of the healer natem. It seemed as if I had found myself in a place somewhere between the world of the senses and intuitive understanding. I'd left the normal waking state. I had done so several times before, but not like this. The idea of expansive states that happened simultaneously, and in different times...Frankly, I was dumbstruck. What was the reality of what I had experienced? I didn't know. But I felt that the event was rare and important, with a significance for my life that I didn't yet understand.

As my body returned to me, I felt slight and giddy. I looked over at Raphael, who was sleeping like a baby. Cici gave me an intent, puzzled look. But I had no comments to make or thoughts to offer. The rest of the night was a blur.

My body needed to rest, and the need seemed to be related to the possession. I heard the echoing of the Indians vomiting before sleeping. I felt I couldn't muster up the energy to drink guayusa, but Carlos insisted that I must. I performed the function as quickly as I could, almost like a zombie. When I'd cleared myself out fully, I found a secluded spot on the beach among the boulders.

I spread a plastic garbage bag on the ground as my bedding and stretched out on it. Underneath me I could feel the hard-shelled spiders crawling. I sat up and watched their tunneling bodies, moving ridges in the plastic. Then I lay back down, too tired to think. I felt the animalitos like rocks, beating into my back. They moved up and down my spine. I was so exhausted that I convinced myself they would not bite through the flimsy plastic. The animalitos passed back and forth, dozens of them kneading into my back. I didn't care.

I covered myself with my sleeping bag, mostly to keep out the sun that would soon be up. Suddenly, the sky hurled a ferocious rain that fell straight down, as if a pounding waterfall had been let loose. My covering was soaked and I was freezing and chattering. *My God*, I thought, *even with this insane misery I couldn't be more content. Nothing can take away the magic of the night.* Carlos slid under the bag and lay next to me and I slept.

PART THREE

PARTNERSHIP

CHAPTER TWENTY-FIVE

Flechas

After the ceremony on the sacred island, I went back to the States, but over the winter and spring, I returned to Santa Marta several times. Carlos and I continued to perform ceremonies together, and I continued learning and walking along the Red Path.

Carlos had urged me to bring him north, so he could share his knowledge with Americans and raise money to fund his healing work in Ecuador. In the late spring of 2001 we went to the United States Embassy in Quito, where we fought with immigration officials who told us that no one who didn't own property or have a car, a bank account, and a job could enter the United States even on a short tourist visa.

"This man is a spiritual leader for his people," I argued. "I've yet to see a car drive through the jungle or hear of a mortgage on a palm shack. He has several speaking engagements in the States." This was partly true; I'd begun making arrangements for ayahuasca rituals we would hold in New York City.

Somehow, the miraculous occurred: I managed to get Carlos a multi-entry visa that would allow him to come to the States for a period of five years. Perhaps Uwinsut or his powerful legions of spirits had a hand in cutting through the red tape, but I had also called politicians in New York who wrote letters on Carlos's behalf.

As friends I'd told about my experiences shared the stories with others, ever-widening circles of people in New York had heard about my work with Carlos and were eager to meet him and participate in ceremonies. I felt confident that Americans were ready to receive the benefits ayahuasca had to offer.

Aboriginal wisdom was disappearing around the globe. I felt a responsibility to help keep it alive. In my experience, *la medicina sagrada* was a source of wise counsel and spiritual authority that revealed a way of living a healthy life in harmony with nature and one another. It was a counterbalance to our rational, technologically driven, divorced-from-nature kind of life. I wanted to keep learning from it and share it with others.

I had seen in my time in the jungle that Carlos wanted us to be better caretakers of the earth. He clearly saw that Western civilization was driving our planet toward disaster. He did not feel that ancient knowledge should be pitted against modern technology, but that we should embrace the benefits of both. I felt it was crucial that this knowledge, and this balance, not be lost.

The magnitude of what I felt when I was in trance, in ecstatic rapture with the spirits of the cosmos, constituted both a privilege and a duty. I was excited that Carlos and I were a team and that we were bringing the sacred medicine north. Little did I know what the journey would do to us.

Carlos boarded a plane bound for Kennedy Airport in March 2001. As he broke through the crowd coming from baggage claim, I ran up to him and we hugged like long-lost familiars. Carlos's wide eyes explored my face excitedly. He sashayed around the airport like a kid in a candy store, saying what a miracle it was to be standing in Los Estados Unidos. He was raring to go, ready to begin our new adventure.

We carried his luggage to a waiting taxi. His bags, I knew, were filled with ceremonial objects, herbs, and ayahuasca. "Did anything happen at Customs?" I asked. Yes, he told me. The dogs had trotted over to his bags while immigration officials stood by. But the dogs had loved Carlos so much that they just wanted to play with him. They gave the bags only a cursory sniff and Carlos was whisked through without incident.

The cab driver spied on us in the rearview mirror as we raced through late-night Queens into Brooklyn, holding hands and chatting excitedly in Spanish. Then Carlos quieted, looking perplexed. "Why are all the trees dead?" he asked me.

I thought he'd asked where all the trees were. "Ah! The city isn't known for growing trees."

"No, why are they dead?"

I looked around and saw short spindly things, poor excuses for trees, encased in iron fencing. "Carlos, in the North we have seasons. Now the trees are sleeping. Soon buds will sprout and leaves will come."

I thought Carlos would be excited to see famous sites. I pointed out the World Trade Center and the Empire State Building. He'd never heard of them. New York held no glitter or glamour in Carlos's eyes. He knew nothing about the New York Stock Exchange, the Knicks at Madison Square Garden, the Metropolitan Opera or the Metropolitan Museum of Art, or films like *The Lord of the Rings*. He'd never heard of the Beatles or Elvis. *I have an Amazonian warrior with me who has absolutely no relation to our civilization,* I thought. *He's a tabula rasa.*

The taxi dropped us off in lower Manhattan at my friend Barbara's loft in the financial district. As we ate and drank wine with her and her jazz trumpeter boyfriend, Carlos relaxed, broadened his smile, and charmed his hosts. Here, he felt safe.

We had pitched a tent in Barbara's loft for Carlos and me to sleep in. Living in the jungle had toughened me, and I no longer needed the comfort of a cushy double bed, though I'd never reject one. Sleeping in the tent with Carlos was fun, bringing back memories of being a kid on a camping trip and knowing that the next day would be full of excitement. It also gave us the privacy to explore the sexual heat that flowed between us.

Our first ayahuasca ceremony was set for the next day. In the morning, Carlos and I went to a man named Dennis's SoHo loft, where the ceremony would be held that night. Carlos wanted to make sure that everything was set up properly. He urgently felt it was important to get the right supplies to help the people who wanted to experience this new and different practice, many of whom were ailing in one way or another.

So after a brief visit with Dennis, Carlos and I took the elevator back down ten floors to the street and plunged into the melee. I shepherded him through the concrete colossus of the city, leading him through my jungle as he had once led me through his.

Carlos seemed adaptable, but he was hardly undemanding. "Margarita, I've got to have *ruda*," he insisted. "The herbs from my country are what I need. You've got to find them for me." This turned out to be impossible. I found no ruda that was adequate—but not for lack of trying.

We went to Spanish botanicas for herbs, then to hardware stores for candles, ropes, buckets, and garbage pails to hold the purgative guayusa, which we would make in hundred-gallon batches. Carlos complained about the quality of the herbs, the fact that we couldn't find certain herbs he said we had to have, and the low energy and the "negative" chaos on the streets with their bustling crowds. He must have been going through intense culture shock.

Suddenly, on the Lower East Side, I lost Carlos. I backtracked and found him staring at a shrunken head in a storefront window.

The head was small, black and palm-sized, with long black hair. Gutting thread had been used to stitch shut the eyes and mouth. Tsantsa. Only Carlos could sniff out something like this in New York!

Finally we caught the 7 train to Queens. Sitting in the subway car, Carlos started teaching me more about *flechas*—the magical healing arrows that live inside the uwishin's body.

Carlos had told me in Ecuador that he had many types of flechas inside him that came from the sun, moon, lightning, stones, trees, various animals, and spirits. One could receive flechas from natural elements, like plants, waterfalls, and animals such as the jaguar, or from a mentor. When I received flechas, they would come from his personal arsenal.

"Flechas are drawn up from my chest into my mouth, and an element like a tongue captures the sickness within the patient," he said. "I have to ingest the sickness, or bad flechas, grab them in my hands, and disperse them into space with my breath. If I can't remove the patient's dart from inside me after the extraction, I will die. This is the most dangerous feat a healer performs."

Carlos had said that when he removed flechas from patients, he found many types and shapes: some were circles, some crystals, some shafts. He kept the good ones and incorporated them into his arsenal. Those that caused sickness he first attacked with the shiri-shiri leaves and tobacco smoke, which lulled the magic darts lodged in a patient so that they lost power and were easier to remove. I realized that this was what Carlos had been doing when I'd seen him sucking on patients, including the infant Juank, who had made such a remarkable recovery from his head injury.

Sunlight streamed into the subway car. We had reached the elevated track, which meant we'd soon be getting off in Jackson Heights. On one side of Roosevelt Avenue is Little India, and on the other, Little Colombia, where English is rarely spoken. Over half the population in Jackson Heights are immigrants. One shop owner advertised that he sold "Puerto Rican, Mexican, Colombian,

Ecuadorian, Peruvian, Argentinean, Guatemalan, Brazilian, Dominican, Middle Eastern, Greek, and Kosher Foods."

As Carlos and I passed through crowds of Latinos, it felt as if we could have been on a street in Quito or Bogotá. Carlos smiled and made small talk with passersby, delighted that he could converse with neighborly amigos.

We had most of what we needed, but we were looking for aguardiente. We headed for *La Risraralda* market, the last place I could think of that might sell 150-proof cane liquor. We came close; we ended up buying a 100-proof bottle of aguardiente imported from Colombia, the strongest available in the States. Then it was time to get back on the subway for the long ride back to Dennis's place, because we still had to make barrels of guayusa for the night's ritual.

Once we were back on the train, Carlos returned to the flechas. "When you are ready, I will give them to you," he said. "But, Margarita, flechas are like wild dogs—they don't like to be sent to new places. You need power to hold them inside you or they will return to me. If I gave them to you and you were not in complete control, they'd explode inside you and kill you instantly. I am responsible for your safety. Your power is growing, but you need to be completely prepared to overcome and dominate these powers."

The train whooshed down into the tunnel. The bags of aguardiente and herbs were at our feet. People reading newspapers in half a dozen languages got on and off the train. I thought they were fortunate not to be preoccupied with magical arrows that lived inside the body that could explode and kill you if you weren't prepared.

CHAPTER TWENTY-SIX

The *Dueño* of New York

ennis's penthouse overlooked SoHo rooftops and water towers. The view was flat and colorless. Even though I knew this was a chi-chi loft in a coveted area, I yearned for the fertile earth of the jungle as the ritual participants settled down on cushions in a circle in the big open room, stripped of the expensive furniture and rugs it had held a few hours before. There were seventeen people in all; the group included psychiatrists, writers, artists, lawyers, and academics, aged from early twenties to midseventies. They sat facing Carlos, alert, each with a newly purchased bucket by his or her side. Little did they know what the buckets were for.

I had determined after speaking to friends that new-age healers were charging $200 or even more per person per session. Carlos and I thought the price was outrageous, so we came up with $150 for an all-night ceremony. We felt this was fair compensation for airfare, food, lodging, and the difficulty of bringing ayahuasca from South America. There was talk that any amount less than $150 would give people the idea that the work was not valuable. I thought that strange. We had people who really needed help but were poor. They paid little or nothing to participate.

Most of the money we did collect was going toward a great dream of Carlos's, one he and I had discussed at length in the jungle: a way to work with modern medicine in tandem with the wisdom of plants and spirits. "I want to have a healing hospital in the jungle where anyone can come for treatment," Carlos had said to me. "You and I will run the operation. We'll have beds and my medicine garden. We will take care of patients and make them well. They can stay and work with us when they are healed.

"I want to bring scientists there so that we can exchange our expertise and have the best medicines available. Those patients who can pay will pay. Those who cannot, have no fear, for I will help them."

Carlos was dressed to the nines in Shuar costume and his fanciest feathers. His demeanor, sincerity, and charisma enthralled all the New Yorkers. He was an enticing spider drawing in his prey with glistening splendor and promises of the exotic. He explained the process each person would undergo, what each one could expect, and spoke of unlocking the portal gate to the world of spirit. He described the potency and health one could expect from communing with ayahuasca. I watched the listeners' faces, trying to imagine what they were making of it all.

We had already had to explain to Dennis, a journalist who'd done his own experimenting with mind-altering substances, that ayahuasca was not a drug, but a medicinal plant with a healing spirit. The indigenous tribes of the Amazon did not imbibe natem in search of a "high" as Western culture understands it. Using the sacred medicine for escape, relaxation, or experimentation was foreign to them.

"I know from my experience that drugs and ayahuasca are not the same," I'd told Dennis. "Drugs may cause you to hallucinate, or illuminate things for you, but they're not imbued with a nonphysical spirit as ayahuasca is. Hallucinations, by their very definition, are not real. But when one drinks ayahuasca, what one sees is real."

I don't recall any spectacular healings in the first ceremony. I do remember that it was my responsibility to get all the participants to vomit. They behaved worse than I had when I first faced purging. They were resistant and horrified. But I wouldn't let them leave the ritual until they threw up in their buckets. I was a tyrant, just as Carlos had been to me. "Vomit," I insisted over and over. A few people became so obstreperous that I went to Carlos. "You make them do it!" he said. "You know how important it is. That's your job!"

So I kept insisting, and eventually everyone drank the guayusa and purged. One man continued vomiting for over eight hours. He was so sick that I felt sorry for him. Horrendous energy was coming out of him, both spiritual and physical, so that both Carlos and I avoided him until he was well cleaned out.

I looked through the picture window onto the night sky. New York felt oppressive. The water towers mocked me. The jungle was calling to me as people lolled on the polished floor. Some were singing, others were crying. Several candles were lit in the loft; otherwise it was dark. Everyone seemed small against the white walls. And there was Carlos at the head of the room. He could have been on the Pastaza or Bomboiza River. He could have been at the sacred island or on the peaks of the Andes. He could have been in a cave or behind a waterfall as he sang heartily to give life to the ritual.

A woman in her sixties heaved explosively and her false teeth shot into her bucket of vomit. I walked over to help her. "Leave me alone," she snapped, angry and embarrassed. I carefully took her teeth out of the slime, washed them in the kitchen sink, and came back to her. By this time, I could see that she was caught up in a developing vision. I helped place her teeth back in her mouth.

The toilet had overflowed. People were beating on the bathroom door to get in, but others had bad diarrhea and wouldn't come out. One man had to get to the toilet but couldn't stand up on his own, so I helped him. He weighed easily 250 pounds. He leaned on me; I shuffled along the floor, bearing his weight. I got him inside the bathroom, helped him remove his trousers, and left him until he was ready to get back to the ceremony. These tough New Yorkers were humbled and horrified but unable to stop what was happening to them. They begged for it to stop. Some of them cried.

I was very full of ayahuasca myself, and I was literally running all night. I helped Carlos on individual patients and watched everyone like a hawk at the same time. I looked into people's buckets to see if there were any problems significant enough to report to Carlos. There was thick mucus in some of the vomit, bubbling foam and parasites, and some vomit held food particles even though people had been told to fast the day of the ceremony. I noted everything, volume, contents, consistency, stringy vomit, and bitter smells. What the bucket held could suggest many things: gall bladder disease, a poorly functioning liver, uric acid poisoning, gastroenteritis, ulcerations, infections, intestinal obstructions, kidney problems, even cancer. I did not have the scope to understand as well as Carlos what the particles signified, but could "feel" what much of it meant, and I brought to his attention anything that I felt was unusual.

When the ceremony was finally over around ten in the morning, Dennis's loft was a mess. The toilet had to be unclogged, the buckets had to be poured out, and everything had to be cleaned up. Carlos, Dennis, and I went to work because we had to be ready for another wave of all-night ritual participants that evening. When we finished, Carlos got into Dennis's shower. He didn't know how to work it. I helped him.

"Margarita, I don't like these showers you have in America," he said. "The hot water causes energy depletion in my body. I can only be touched by cold water." So I showed him how to make the water ice cold. I wondered why he didn't marvel that water could come from a spigot. Modern conveniences didn't seem to warrant much of his attention.

Before we drifted off to sleep in Dennis's spare room, Carlos told me about the vision he'd had during the ritual.

"The *dueño* [owner] of New York is a giant vampire bat with large black wings," he said. "Its wingspan is so great that it covers the entire city. I watched as it hovered over New York, landed, and sucked energy from the sleeping inhabitants. The vampire reared up at dawn and flew back to its family nest far away from here, in an unpopulated area in the northern heavens."

When we rose from bed about four that afternoon to get ready for the next ritual, Carlos said, "This New York is not a healthy place."

Carlos didn't hesitate to let me know that just about anything that had to do with our culture was harmful to his body. He complained about the poor quality of our food. I agreed. Compared to the fresh and unadulterated food in Ecuador, American food was the equivalent of eating plastic. In Ecuador, people had fewer food choices, but everything they ate was organic.

When we went into restaurants, Carlos was outraged at food left on plates. He'd walk from table to table in disgust at what people had left untouched. He looked into garbage bins behind restaurants and raged at the waste. I understood, because there are many starving children in Ecuador.

Carlos didn't navigate well in my world. Because he didn't speak English, I spoke and listened for him. He couldn't drive a car. He didn't know the streets of New York. He didn't know how to do anything that I took for granted. It was like leading a child, a wild child, step by step. His squabbling was frustrating and could be tiresome, but I was also amused at his reactions, and we continued bonding. All the time I was learning from him and watching miraculous healings. But I began to worry that New York really might not be a healthy place for him. "Margarita," he said to me one day as we prepared for another ayahuasca ceremony in Dennis's loft, "my guardians are always protecting me. But the energy is so weak in New York that it is not easy for me to renew my power."

CHAPTER TWENTY-SEVEN

A Poultice of Tar

C arlos and I worked around the clock, treating people in groups and one on one. One harrowing evening as we worked on an asthmatic who had been diagnosed in childhood, Carlos sucked in the sickness. He couldn't dislodge the bad flecha from his throat, and he began to choke. I spontaneously grabbed him and with much grappling, using the condor fan, aguardiente, prayers, and spirit helpers, I evicted the thing.

After this episode, Carlos and I began using a different technique on asthma patients. We stripped a turkey feather to the quill, wrapped it with a small cotton swab, and dipped it into aguardiente and freshly grated ginger. Carlos would ease the twelve-inch-long feather into the patient's windpipe, past the vocal cords, and into the bronchial tubes at the top of the lungs where he swabbed the mixture. Carlos explained that the bacteria that lived in the bronchial tubes were very difficult to kill, even with antibiotics. In his practice, he had found that putting an antiseptic directly onto the juncture with the lungs did the trick. In each case the asthma subsided.

He told me that he could cure tuberculosis by catching an

uninjured vulture. It had to have at least a five-foot wingspan. "Vultures have seven different types of curative properties and can be used for seven different ailments," he said. "The vulture must be killed by tranquilizing, not violence. For tuberculosis, the patient must drink the fresh vulture blood and be encased in the bird's warm carcass overnight."

I never got to see this in action, but I did see plenty of "unbelievable" cures at work. I saw Carlos set a man's shattered leg—a leg that the doctors said needed several operations and pins to hold the bones in place—by using plasters of herbs and ayahuasca. After two months the man's leg was healed and he walked without a limp. No surgery. I was not readily going to discount the vulture-blood cure.

Although our ceremonies in New York were successful, I felt disconnected. New York, with its concrete, glass, steel, electric power, and tall buildings that made a human being feel like an ant in a dark crevice, seemed to generate a life-sucking energy. I missed the jungle ceremonies; the white man's world seemed drier, less juicy, less alive. Carlos hated the city and begged me to get him to the countryside, so I set up several ceremonies in Upstate New York, New Jersey, and Pennsylvania. We left town on an Amtrak train and Carlos began to breathe more easily.

In the Hudson Valley, I found Carlos a place to stay at my friend Jeanne's. I stayed at Gray Cottage, a couple of miles away.

Miles knew that Carlos and I were lovers; I had told him. He never said, "Come back to me." He just removed himself from my life. We both knew we were heading for a divorce, but I had been away so much that we hadn't had time to talk about initiating the process.

Manon came home from boarding school for the summer and kept to a rigorous practice schedule on the piano. We'd spend an intimate day or two talking, working, cooking, or just being together, then I wouldn't see her for days.

In July I taught in a graduate music program for a month and I lived at Gray Cottage while I worked twelve-hour days at school. Manon and Miles accepted my absences and returns with a resigned equanimity, as they had when I was away in the jungle. Miles began dating.

I still valued the teaching I was doing, but my composing career was in shambles. I was moving in a different direction and I was completely committed and engaged. I'd found my lineage, and in a sense my home, which was on the move with Carlos.

I would visit him in lodgings I had set up for him. In the beginning, he accepted my absences too. One day at Jeanne's house, Carlos and I stood in her lovely guest room, which overlooked fields that rolled down to the Hudson River. Carlos discovered that a bee had found its way into the room.

"It can't find its way out," he said. "It's dancing, looking for flowers and water to drink. Here's another one lying down, suffering from thirst, but there is no water here." Carlos picked up the bees and a few of their companions and released them outside one by one so that they could "feed and fly free."

"Margarita, we must collect dew for the bees that find themselves here when I am not around to help them," Carlos said. He was like that. He loved and cared for every creature. I adored his innocence.

But after a time, Carlos became frustrated with me for not being with him. He wanted me with him at all times but that simply was not possible with my teaching schedule. I couldn't let him come and live at Gray Cottage! Instead, I found people to help him while I was at school.

One weekend, Carlos told me he'd seen Miles and Manon in a vision during one of the ceremonies.

"Margarita, your husband loves you very much," he said. "You must be kind to him and your daughter."

The vision stunned and hurt me. I knew Carlos was right. I

loved my daughter and she knew it, but I wasn't around a lot that summer. I loved Miles, too, but for all the pain it caused, I could not continue the life we had once had together. When my teaching job was over, despite the sorrow I felt about my family life, I continued working with Carlos.

The word was beginning to spread that Carlos an authentic shaman and that he was willing to share his knowledge with the white man. To many Americans, Carlos was like a guru, and some people lost their heads and followed him around like groupies. His healing powers were as great as ever, and he was kind to everyone he had contact with. But he was reveling in all the attention he was getting, and I began to understand that being accepted by North Americans conferred a kind of legitimacy on him that he found thrilling.

As summer progressed, our ayahuasca began to run out. We had to mix tobacco juice with it, but its effects were still viable. By this time I was drinking several portions each session. My body could handle it, and I was capable of taking good care of patients as well as delving deeper into the spirit world. The ayahuasca spirit was teaching me personal songs for healing that I would sing the way Carlos did.

During rituals, Carlos showed me how to observe the way tobacco smoke curled and circulated over a patient. If the smoke sat there, not rising, negative energy was keeping it down. We'd watch the smoke as it swirled around a patient's head to determine the kind of *limpia* (cleansing) we would have to do.

"An apprentice learns by being attentive and alert, watching carefully," Carlos said. "Margarita, those who ask questions obtain information, but it is not engraved in their minds and they lose the information quickly."

We worked with Cary, a middle-aged woman with spina bifida. When she was nine years old, her leg had been amputated above her knee because it was growing too slowly. She had lost a kidney;

her bladder was inflamed and she was on antibiotics. Nonetheless, she had an open, oozing sore on her amputated leg. She told us her doctors thought that infection occupied 95 percent of what remained of her leg. They couldn't control the systemic infection that she had sustained for years, and she was about to lose her second kidney.

The pus coming from the leg infection was thick and whitish in color. Carlos and I prepared numerous bowls of tobacco in a pipe, pouring thick clouds of smoke over the open wound, where it formed a resinous layer that clung to the flesh. It took a very long time to create enough resin to cover the sore—all the smoking made me nauseated and dizzy. Tobacco resin dripped and oozed; we couldn't see the wound because of all the smoke surrounding it. The syrupy smoke irritated my eyes and made me choke; it was so viscous that I couldn't see the walls of the room. But finally the lesion was covered with a thick layer of resin, a stronger killer of viruses and bacteria than pharmaceuticals.

Closing off the wound created pressure in the leg. The next day, craters of pus erupted from new holes on Cary's thigh. They looked awful, but they allowed the infection to dissipate. Each day, new ruptures appeared. But eventually the leg healed.

I'd been warning Carlos that what we were doing in America was illegal, because ayahuasca is classified as a drug in this country, and that we had to keep our ceremonies secret. Carlos didn't really understand this. His work came by the grace of God. He told me a story.

"I was in Quito doing a healing when two police officers came up to me and asked for my permit to doctor. 'My permit for what?' I said. 'Do you know the knowledge of uwishins? Do we need permission to learn the knowledge that comes from the Great Spirit?'

"Margarita, they wanted to arrest me for practicing medicine without a license. I asked them, 'If someone is sick or dying, you're saying that I need permission to help this person? Does a mathematician working in theories need a permit? Why would this be so?'

"Finally, one of the policemen said that his wife was very sick and asked me if I could heal her. He wanted to know if I could guarantee a cure. I replied: 'Will you guarantee you will pay me?' So I went with them and cured his wife. I never have trouble because what I do comes from the highest power."

"So did the policeman pay you, Carlos?"

"*Sí.*"

CHAPTER TWENTY-EIGHT

A Different Kind of Power

By midsummer, I was getting calls from as far away as California asking if Carlos and I were available to travel and lead ceremonies. But New York held new complications. Almost overnight, Carlos had become a sensation. He had money. People loved him. And the work was going stupendously well.

By charging people $150 per ceremony, Carlos was amassing a small fortune. He was paying me a salary and putting the rest into savings for the hospital to be built in Morona Santiago. Carlos had people running around looking for more money to fund the endeavor. I didn't think any donor or any organization was going to put up big money for Carlos's hospital, but with the ceremonies we were doing all right financially.

After ayahuasca rituals, he would spread out hundreds of dollars on the beds of friends' homes, counting it over and over, his eyes shining. In Ecuador, his people—this formerly proud warrior class—are treated as second-class citizens, and their circumstances are desperate. He had seen his people succumb to illness and starvation. Now he wanted success and wealth. How could he not?

At the same time, Carlos was inviting others to share in learning healing techniques. People took him seriously. They wanted to be his helpers. Chiropractors, Reiki healers, and others were thrilled to be at his side while he worked over patients. Each one of them felt special, singled out. Carlos made everyone feel that way. In rituals, he poured everything he had into his patients. His love flowed clearly as a powerful waterfall, and that was the most compelling reason that people wanted to follow him and help him help others.

Although I cared deeply for the sick we tended to, I was liking the American ceremonies less and less: the stench of vomit in enclosed spaces, the exhaustion after the dusk-till-dawn healings, the constant responsibility for others and their needs, and the clinging of those who wanted to be around Carlos. I couldn't help thinking about how the best healers avoid codependency with their patients, something these Americans made very difficult. Americans needed much more attention than the Shuar. They felt they deserved it.

Carlos as a healer is incomparable, magnificent. In hindsight, though, it was difficult being with him when so many people wanted to be in his presence, to give him gifts and money.

I only wanted to tend to people who were sick, and several of our patients were very ill. We worked tirelessly with them during the day as well as in the evening rituals. There were people at our ceremonies who were *not* sick but still wanted one-on-one attention from Carlos, which they got. But some never seemed to get enough care and tending. "Me. Me. Me."

Then one night Carlos said to me, "I love you deeply. But there is your house, your family, and we are not living together. We will, in another place and time. I have visions of us in Canada."

"I love you too," I said, "but I've heard you slept with other women while I was away."

"You are the one I love," he said.

"Then why am I hearing these things?"

"I thought you didn't care about me anymore," he said, looking hurt. I shouldn't have left him on his own. I would come to learn that he felt my absence as an indication that I didn't care enough to keep him at my side. The issues that came up for us were not uncommon, but because of our cultural differences, our interpretations of events were drastically different. I was disappointed with Carlos's fascination with American riches and women, whether I had a right to judge him or not. Perhaps he was disappointed in me too. But then he said, "You are my wife. You don't ever want to leave me."

I was dreaming constantly during this time. I dreamed Carlos cut his hair, wore Western clothes, and got a real job. I didn't recognize him.

"Why don't you know me?" he asked.

"How could you?" I responded, thinking, I really don't like Carlos now that he is one of them. He looked like a greaser. I berated him in the dream; I said, "You're not Shuar anymore."

In another dream I saw him climbing buildings at night. Carlos was a dark thief, a cat burglar. I caught him many times, although others were unaware that he was a robber. I never told the others but he knew that I knew.

And I dreamed of my husband. We bought a house near the ocean. The owners came to take the furniture away. The last thing to go was my piano. I realized that the table was gone. Everything. There was nothing to sit on. It seemed too late in the season to plant a garden.

I was making judgments in my dreams and rearranging my feelings while I slept. I had strong and tender emotions for Miles; we'd had twenty years together, and I was teetering on waves of disappointment in Carlos. But still he was a luminous, magnificent healer, unparalleled. He'd turn and smile, telling me how much he loved me, and I knew that it was true. Our work was strong, and we were helping people.

In early August, Carlos and I drove to a retreat center in Pennsylvania where he was scheduled to talk about Shuar healing and meet with Native Americans. He desperately wanted to meet his "brothers and sisters," as he put it, from the North. The original people.

We stayed several days with First Nation people from Canada. Four Grandmother Elders from the Anishnaabek clan wanted Carlos to perform healings on them at the lodge we stayed in, but the owner, worried about the legal implications, would not allow a ceremony. So the Elders, who were quite taken with Carlos, asked us to come to their reserve in Canada to heal their people.

"So many of our people are sick and dying," they said. We readily agreed to go to them. I took the Grandmothers' information and gave them my phone number. The Elders would meet with the chief and council of their tribe to secure the money needed for our flights to Canada.

Carlos and I returned to New York, and we decided that he should go to fetch more sacred medicine in Ecuador. He was going home a wealthy man by the standards of his country. The ceremonies we had conducted had brought in thousands of dollars. Wealth equaled power, but this power was different from that which he already held within his breast—the power of healing and love.

At Kennedy Airport, I stood at the ticket counter while Carlos paid an astronomical fee for excess baggage. He had purchased Tibetan singing bowls for healing. He'd received expensive gifts from patients. And he had bought things for his family: irons, high-heeled shoes, short-wave radios, and a four-track music recording system. He even wanted to buy a washing machine! So many things held him in thrall: video games, dolls for the girls, a microscope for his son. We both knew that the money had been meant for his healing hospital in the jungle.

I began to believe that Carlos had lost his balance in our materialistic culture. But then I realized that it was his innocence, not his balance, that had been damaged. I'd brought him from a land where hard cash was difficult to come by. Family, love, healing, honor, and friendship were the accepted currency, not money. And suddenly, I felt bad that I had brought Carlos to America.

"Carlos, have you put away money for the hospital?" I asked.

"Yes. I have some for that," he said, "but Margarita, when I come back we will make all the money we need. We are just beginning."

With Carlos gone, my day-to-day life resumed, all too real. My marriage was over, and I left Gray Cottage. I'd rented a small house, a quiet place in the country, and I lived there by myself. I thought about the whirlwind Carlos had swept me up in since I first knew him. It had been both exciting and addicting. And I realized that I'd thrown Carlos into a similar vortex of scintillation when I brought him to America. He'd gotten shaken up pretty hard.

I dreamed that I returned to Ecuador. Alone. I thought to myself: *I am a wise woman. I must go to the spiritual well I discovered deep inside me. There perhaps I will find answers.* The truth was so big it was written on my inner parts. I could sense other people's problems and I was aware of the power and energy that came inside me to help me do this. Carlos had kept telling me to pray to the Great Spirit, to petition for grace while doing this sacred work. He trusted me completely, as I trusted him. "You get the message of my truth, love, and healing," he said.

I was trying to understand what had happened to me and where it would lead. I knew I would have to take the gift I had learned from Carlos and not confuse *it* with *him*. At the same time, I would hold a clear image of him as an honorable, compassionate teacher who initiated me in ways that I would never forget.

I had gone to Ecuador to get healed. Carlos had saved my life. He led me on an incredible journey through the jungle. He joined me in a powerful energy exchange. He gave and gave to me: secret teachings, health, sacred knowledge. In the process of assisting

Carlos, I'd had an unveiling of my own power. I'd been reinvented, remade. I wasn't sure if I would ever settle into that new way of being, but I knew the path I was on. I'd learned that there was a strong healer archetype working through me. My happiness was rooted in healing work.

I wanted to keep accessing Carlos's wisdom, but I didn't want a life that would orbit around him. Continuing with Carlos, which I was prepared to do, could lead to brilliance or to terrible danger. Though I was fascinated with him and his world, part of me was trying to slow down and stay balanced. But I knew our paths were still intertwined. We weren't finished—not by a long shot.

CHAPTER TWENTY-NINE

The Bay of Beavers

arlos and I spoke several times while he was in Ecuador preparing medicines to bring to Canada. Even though I was unsure about our future together, I was excited to work with him again. Dorothy K. called me from the Wikwemikong Health Center on Manitoulin Island, Canada, where we would be working. She was overseeing travel and housing arrangements for Carlos and me. I had to coordinate our plans and make arrangements with her, with Carlos in Ecuador, and with the Canadian Embassy in Quito.

Even though the Grandmothers had instructed her to get Carlos and me into Canada at all costs, Dorothy had concerns. She wanted to know if Carlos had ever taken advantage of his position or his power. Was he safe with patients? She mentioned other medicine men she had known who had violated women and taken advantage of naïve patients. I assured her Carlos was not that kind of healer.

"Carlos is meticulous," I told her. "He is devoted to his patients. He is conscientious and heals with prayer and love."

Still, the back-and-forth continued. I e-mailed Dorothy: "Carlos is bringing a document from the Shuar-Achuar Federation declaring his stature to use sacred ceremonial plants and religious objects in the healings. His people certify him. Carlos uses plants from the Amazon, spiritual teachings, and hands-on healing in the way of the Shuar. He will tell your people about his culture, language, medicine, music, dance, and the arts of his people.

"It is the Grandmothers who insist Carlos and I be invited to your community to conduct healings. And as you mentioned in an earlier e-mail, our trip and expenditure has been authorized by the chief of your people."

Carlos and I planned to fly to Canada from New York City, but then came September 11, 2001. Air traffic was suspended for three days, and Carlos was stuck in Ecuador. The Wikwemikong Council sent a new air ticket to Quito for Carlos to fly directly to Canada. They also sent a ticket for Mauro, whom they'd quickly invited at Carlos's suggestion, and who would never have been able to fly into the States without a visa. The Grandmothers insisted that Carlos and I had to come right away. They didn't care how much the tickets cost. My flight to Sudbury, Canada, was the very next day. Our plan was to spend three weeks with the Elders of the Anishnaabek tribe.

I arrived in Sudbury, in northern Ontario, after changing planes in Toronto. Carlos and Mauro had presumably already landed, but my plane was hours late. I picked up my baggage from the carousel. Where were Carlos and Dorothy? I called the phone number I had been given in Manitoulin. No one answered. I waited and waited.

Given that I was the only traveler in the airport, it was not hard for Dorothy to spot me when she finally arrived, several hours later. Dorothy was Anishnaabek. She was overweight, dressed in sweat pants and a sweatshirt, and she smoked long filtered cigarettes. Her eyes were almond-shaped and she looked like she had Inuit blood.

(I would learn from the Elders that Great Spirit had told aboriginals from the Bering Strait to make their home on Manitoulin Island.) A thick black braid rode down her back. She seemed tough and awesome in size, but her voice was so soft it was barely audible. Her round face had an unhealthy pallor.

"Dorothy, did Carlos and Mauro arrive?" I asked.

She stamped out her cigarette, apologizing for being so late, and began walking out of the airport terminal. I followed her, carrying my bags. She hadn't answered my question, and I began wondering if something had gone seriously awry.

Then Carlos attacked me from behind, giggling as he embraced me. Mauro, who now had a wife and a newborn child in Ecuador, emerged from a van and tackled me too. Though he'd turned twenty since I'd last seen him in Morona Santiago, he barely had enough hair on his face to make a decent moustache.

Dorothy looked at me. "Hum," I could almost hear her think, "you're not Indian, but these guys trust you, so you must be okay." She eased up, becoming friendly because they had shown such delight in my arrival. Also, she needed me to translate what they said.

We all hopped into the big black van for the two-hour ride to Dorothy's hometown, which she called Wiki, on Manitoulin Island. Outside Sudbury, northern Ontario was sparsely populated. As we drove, Mauro pointed to the pristine Precambrian pine forests and crystal lakes, which Dorothy said held frigid, fresh water. Mauro was flying high, excited to be outside Ecuador for the first time. His friends would never have this chance. I saw the idea that he was a man flicker in his eyes. His life was going to be filled with splendid opportunities from here on out. I was proud of him. Such a kid, I thought, but his life with Carlos had given him rare insight into the world.

Great boulders stretched on either side of the highway. On top of them were rock sculptures. They looked like cairns that might have been created to honor the Thunderbirds or other spirit beings that the First Nation People worshiped. There were high plateaus with steep cliffs—a picture-postcard wilderness.

I sat in the front of the van next to Dorothy and translated for all of us, which became overwhelming as everyone insisted on talking about different things at the same time. Dorothy lit another cigarette and told us about Wiki, short for the Wikwemikong Unceded Indian Reserve, which was located on the eastern side of the island.

"Wiki is a First Nations land that has never been ceded to Canada. We have our own government and laws. Ours is the only land in Canada that does not belong to the Canadian government. We never signed a treaty with them.

"The Ojibwa or Faith Keepers, Odawa or Traders, and Pottawatomi or Fire Keepers live on Manitoulin. Their alliance is known as the Three Fires Confederacy—or the Anishnaabek people who speak Anishnabemowin.

"Our people have traditional social gatherings like competition powwows, rain dances, and sweat lodges. During ceremonies we wear ribbon skirts, jingle skirts, beaded buckskin, and moccasins. The Midewiwin, our religious belief and ceremonial practice, is also called the Great Medicine Lodge. It is a secret society that holds the wisdom of our medicine men and the songs, stories, and rituals of our traditional heritage."

After two hours we came to a small town with clapboard houses and a broken-down diner. We crossed a bridge onto Manitoulin Island, the largest freshwater island in the world. The bridge spanned Georgian Bay in Lake Huron. The water looked deep and pure.

It was still daylight as we continued on, passing several small towns. When we got out of the car for a short break, the air was startlingly crisp. We made prayers at the edge of the lake. Carlos pointed overhead where four eagles flew, circling us. He sang and we smoked a pipe among us.

"The locals hunt deer, bear, moose, fish, and beaver here on the island," Dorothy said. "Wikwemikong Bay is known as the Bay of Beavers."

"My father's name in Shuar means beaver," Carlos said.

We got back into the van and traveled on to the Wikwemikong Health Center—a new wooden building shaped like an eagle—where we would perform our ayahuasca ceremonies. Dorothy showed us around the complex. It was designed like an outpatient hospital with examination rooms, dental suites, a wing dedicated to the treatment of diabetes, and a large teepee-shaped room that was used for traditional medicine. The nurses and doctors had gone home for the day, but Ron, a large and unfriendly medicine man, was waiting for us. I saw jealousy painted all over his face. He clearly disliked Carlos, but he showed us herbs and where they were dried and told us about the medicinal plants that grew on the island. Carlos ignored Ron's attitude; he was just fascinated with the information.

Dorothy was proud of the new center because it incorporated indigenous medicine. "Wiki is the first of its kind," Dorothy said. "It combines the best in aboriginal and allopathic medicine. An Indonesian healer visited us last year to share his skills with our doctors and patients. Carlos is the second healer we've invited. We intend to bring medicine men and women from all over the world to exchange traditional healing methods. Our center will be a repository of aboriginal medical knowledge to be shared with everyone." This was a model of what Carlos and I wanted to do with our hospital in Santa Marta.

"Margarita, our liaison with this Nation will bring modern medical technology to the hospital we'll build together in the jungle," Carlos said, excited. "We'll have the kind of exchange I have been striving for."

We said our good-byes to Ron as Dorothy rushed us out the door. We were due at a sweat lodge to welcome us into the community.

Afterward, a feast had been arranged in a private home. The sweat lodge, a low dome made from branches and tarps, was in a field. It was below freezing as twenty of us stripped to thin clothing— we women had to wear long skirts—entered the lodge, and sat in the womblike structure. The medicine man prayed and sang while dousing rocks in a fire pit with water. Steam rose, making it difficult to see or breathe. During four rounds of purification the lodge became hotter and hotter until finally the ceremony concluded.

We dressed and moved on to an old farmhouse feeling cleansed and renewed. In a room that was warm and softly lit, a dozen people waited to greet Carlos, Mauro, and me. We formed a large circle, holding hands as Carlos and the Elders prayed for thirty minutes to plead for healing in the community and to bless the food. We ate venison stew, moose, fry bread, Jell-O, salads, green beans, potatoes, pies, and pastries, washed down with Kool Aid. Dogs barked outside as small children were tucked in bed. The grown-ups, with immense faith in Carlos, discussed the healing that would take place the next day.

Carlos and I hadn't had a chance to talk about anything personal yet. He was as pleased to be alone with me as I was with him. Our passion for each other was still there. As we drove to the house where we would stay, I took the opportunity to ask him how his trip through immigration went.

"I had my documents to bring in the medicines from the Canadian government and the Anishnaabek Tribal Council, as well as my Shuar Federation papers," he said. "Interpol stopped Mauro and me at the airport in Quito. They wanted to know about the ayahuasca and other plants I was taking out of the country, but when I showed them my documents they let us get on the plane. Then I showed my papers in Miami, and we had no trouble there. In Toronto the Canadians asked about the plants. I said they were for healing, and they said, 'Okay, you can take your things, but we are keeping one of your suitcases.' The other three bags I have here." A few days later, the police would deliver the last suitcase to us, intact.

Dorothy dropped us off at the home of one of the Grandmother Elders, Irene, for the night. Grandma Irene had been at the feast and was thrilled that we were staying in her home. "When I came to Pennsylvania to meet Carlos," she said, "we'd had thirty-three deaths that year so far. I was saddened by what was happening to our people in Wiki. There is so much violence, drugs, and alcohol. I knew you had to come. We need you."

Grandma Irene was the top Elder of the Anishnaabek, born in 1926 in Manitoulin. She belonged to the Black Bear Clan. She was a small woman with a hearty laugh and long gray hair that she always wore in a braid, except when she slept. Her hands were thin and somewhat arthritic. When she spoke, everyone listened. She was an eagle feather carrier, a sacred pipe carrier, and a healer. She had several other titles that carried great responsibility for doing the work of the Great Spirit to benefit her people, but those titles I am not allowed to write down.

It was past midnight when we arrived. We set down our suitcases, and then we were summoned to Grandma Irene's altar, where she made a powerful pipe ceremony. By the time she finally led me to my room, I'd been up for twenty-four hours. I hit the bed until morning.

The next morning, Grandma and I sat drinking coffee. Carlos and Mauro made sour faces. They weren't accustomed to coffee, but they did want food. The plates they'd piled high several times the night before hadn't been enough. I'd always wondered how they stayed so trim. When they didn't have to fast for ceremonies, these two ate triple the quantity of food a normal person consumes.

The kitchen door opened and in came Grandma's men friends. They slapped on the table whitefish, northern pike, and walleye fresh from the waters of Lake Huron. While Grandma put the fish in the oven, we got dressed. We had a tight schedule that day. We ate quickly, then headed out by pickup truck to the Wasse Abin High School, a new brick and glass building high in the hills above Wiki, where Carlos would give a talk to the community.

"I have come in answer to a cry for help," Carlos said to a gymnasium packed with high school students, council members, Elders, and schoolchildren. "Your Elders told me that my brothers are sick in the North. I have come to answer the call." As I translated, Carlos talked about the Shuar and sacred medicine. Mauro spoke briefly. Then we answered questions, met with activists in smaller groups, and went into classrooms to talk to students and teachers. Everyone was excited and impressed with Carlos, but soon we had to excuse ourselves to prepare for that night's ceremony at the Wiki Health Center. We'd seen posters up in town that invited everyone in the community to attend.

Dorothy drove us to the center. As we got out of the van, a young Anishnaabek girl approached us. She looked about thirteen years old. "Can I help you?" I asked.

"I…I need to speak to Carlos privately," she stammered.

But before she even formulated her question, Carlos spoke to her in Spanish. I translated his words. "Carlos says you are pregnant."

Her eyes filled with tears. "How does he know?" she cried. "Is he certain?"

"Yes. There is no doubt." I was really curious as to how Carlos could know what this skinny teenager didn't know herself, but only suspected. He went on to explain in Spanish.

"He sees it. He sees the child inside your eyes," I translated. He told me that he could tell by looking into a woman's eyes if she was pregnant. "You must not be afraid to tell your parents," he continued. "Do this tonight. They will forgive you. It will be all right."

Carlos embraced her as she wept. Her friends looked on, not knowing what had taken place. Later that night, several students would come to drink the medicine and she would be one of them.

CHAPTER THIRTY

Medicine of the Stars

We cooked up the ayahuasca and guayusa in the modern kitchen of the health center. It seemed an unusual place to perform our ceremony because it felt so much like a hospital. But if natem was flexible enough to go from the jungle to a fancy Manhattan loft, I figured it would find its place here too.

Dorothy introduced Mauro to a young Portuguese woman named Connie, who would be his personal translator. They seemed to get along famously even though they couldn't converse in Spanish at first. Connie picked up the similarity of Portuguese and Spanish. Soon they managed to understand each other. I could see Mauro fashioning a love affair with her in his mind.

When the four of us walked out into the main room, we found a large, patient crowd of Native Americans milling about. Forty-five people were waiting for healing! The Anishnaabek, as I'd noted the night before, were light-skinned in comparison to Carlos and Mauro. They were dressed in sweatshirts, sweatpants, red-checked hunting shirts, and tennis shoes. The Grandmothers wore skirts and tied their long hair back, roping it around their heads. There were teenagers and families with children there too. They had waited two hours for us to appear.

Carlos wanted to begin the ceremony immediately, but I insisted that he put on his traditional clothes. In ceremonies toward the end of his sojourn in the United States, he'd fallen into the habit of wearing pressed black pants and black leather shoes, very un-uwishin-like to my mind. I suspected that the Anishnaabek needed to see him in his full regalia. While he and Mauro got dressed, I told the crowd a little about Carlos and explained that I was there to help and to translate.

When Carlos appeared with his condor fans, crystals, feathers, and headdress, everyone in the room gasped. Mauro stood behind his father, dressed the same way. They were both bare-chested and barefoot.

I was relieved to see that the Native Americans focused Carlos, brought him back to his old self. Though Carlos's practice was not part of their tradition, they accepted him immediately because he embodied, as they saw it, the holy sacred ways of their Elders: natural living, respect, and love for Mother Earth. He in turn saw the Indians as brothers; he gave of himself without expecting anything in return. They didn't have to pay a cent to come to the healings. The clinic had given Carlos, Mauro, and me each a small stipend for our efforts—nothing like the money that had washed through our hands in New York.

When Carlos finished speaking to the crowd, we lined everyone up to take the ayahuasca from the small seeded cup that Carlos always used, the cup I'd had my first sip from in a time that seemed the distant past. The whole community, including the little ones, swallowed the medicine that Carlos had blessed. No one questioned Carlos's authority. Even though they hadn't heard of ayahuasca before that night, they knew they were drinking sacred medicine. I knew most of them were Catholic; it was like watching them take the holy Eucharist.

But when I looked around at the crowd, I wanted to cry—there was so much suffering. I had never seen so many defeated and gravely ill people in one place. I could see concern on Mauro's face. I didn't think he'd ever handled a crowd like this before. None of us had.

Carlos gave himself, Mauro, and me ayahuasca that only an uwishin uses, a very concentrated form of natem. He called it the Medicine of the Stars. I'd never had it before, and I gulped with trepidation.

"Margarita, I want you to administer ayahuasca and heal people like I do," Carlos said. "I want you to be able to conduct medicine ceremonies on your own. I need to pass on my skills to you." This was a grave responsibility. I wasn't sure I wanted it.

As people waited for the medicine to take effect, the three of us discussed how to proceed. We grouped people according to their illnesses: those who'd told us they were heroin and morphine users close to Carlos on the floor; acute and chronic diabetics together in another area. We had people with wheelchairs and walkers, heart patients, rape victims, two men with broken backs, a husband and wife who'd lost two sons, a man going blind, and an Anishnaabek Elder dressed in full native regalia who was also a deacon in the church. He had diabetes, cancer, and gangrene in both lower legs.

For the one-on-one healing treatment, we decided to break the group into two sections; half would go to Mauro and Connie and half to Carlos and me. By this time thirty minutes had passed and the medicine was beginning to take hold.

Carlos called in the *cascada de luz,* the waterfall of light. The sick rolled from sitting to lying down. They were crying, praying. Throwing up. Having visions. I cleaned them of vomit and urine. A thunderbird the size of a 747 flew low over my head.

While my visions grew, I began to pick up people and bring them to Carlos. I carefully helped the old ones to lie down in front of him. A few feet to the side of us, Mauro and Connie were intently working on a young boy.

I bent over to listen to Carlos's words, and I told him what the people said. It was like being on a battlefield—so up-front, life-or-death absorbing, critical, dangerous, and hopeful. Carlos told me things. "This one will die soon." "We must do something now." "We can save this one." "Ask him why his organ is missing." "What medicine is he taking for his pancreas?"

"This one has a bad heart," Carlos whispered. "But she doesn't know. She knows she's suffering from diabetes. Tell her that I am going to help her get better."

I gazed at Mauro not ten feet away. He looked scared. The stream of patients seemed never-ending; after five hours, they still kept coming. I was too busy to pay much attention. The Medicine of the Stars was powerful.

Frequently, I moved around the room looking for distress signals among my charges. I was reeling and thought I might go down, but I fought it like the devil so I could walk across the room to attend to an eighty-five-year-old woman who was going through a terrible time. She was hard of hearing, frail, and afraid, and she needed help getting up to go to the bathroom. She clutched her purse to her breast and asked me, "Do you speak Indian?"

"No," I replied, unable to say any more. I mustered my strength and lifted her, almost carrying her to the bathroom. We were inside a long time, undressing, sitting, standing, dressing, moving back into the main hall.

Carlos yelled for me to help him with a drug addict on the table, and I left the old lady with the purse. His intensity was brutal during times like this. He was like a machine gun leveled at me. When I misunderstood something, he screamed. He must have been feeling the pressure that healing so many people put on him.

"*Calmate*, Carlos. *Tranquillo*," I finally said. My audacity stunned him, but then he laughed for a long time, and he did relax. He'd understood that we were working together toward the same end. It felt very right being there with him.

Patients continued to come to Carlos and Mauro as morning light broke through the windows. Our work didn't get any easier. I'd never seen a more unhealthy group of people. The three of us were horrified at how many of the women had had hysterectomies. Children had an aggressive form of braces in their mouths that a doctor had told them was needed to set their jaws properly. Several of the men had had their gallbladders removed. It was clear to me that the medical doctors who had been treating this population had been operating indiscriminately. It made me furious and sad. At nine in the morning, everyone left and the nurses and doctors began arriving at the clinic. We'd made intense contact with the people we'd worked on, and they wanted to return that evening for another ceremony. Grandma Irene drove me, Carlos, Mauro, and a teenage girl back to her house so we could rest.

When we got to her place, the others went to bed. The girl who'd been in the car with us pulled me into an unused bedroom. She wanted to talk.

"I have never been able to tell this to anyone," she said, crying. "My father raped me when I was eight. My mother knew but refused to help me. She pretended that it never happened. I had no one to talk to. It went on and on until a year ago. This has been my deepest, darkest secret. I beg you to tell no one."

"You are very brave," I said. "Because you are able to speak of this thing that has been festering inside you for seven years, you are going to be able to heal and move on with your life."

"The medicine healed me," the girl said. "I could never face this until last night." I sat with her for several hours as she cried.

And so it went on and on and on. Every night more people would arrive at the Wiki Center for healings. They came from as far away as Thunder Bay and Sault Ste. Marie, two hundred miles away. Word traveled fast and we had patients day and night. By the end of our three weeks in Wiki, we would see almost three hundred people.

CHAPTER THIRTY-ONE

The Quill

At Grandma Irene's we were intimately involved in the daily life of the community. We saw patients who came to the house for follow-up treatment, and we observed many improvements. Grandma Irene, who was an insulin-dependent diabetic like many of her relatives and friends, checked her blood daily. After the first night of ayahuasca, she needed only half her usual dose of injected insulin! The same thing was true of all the diabetics we treated. We made energy drinks from Carlos's healing recipes to help them regain their strength, and we gave them sorely needed lessons in nutrition. Our patients were not allowed to go to the grocery store to buy the sodas, chips, donuts, and fried foods that they were used to. Carlos changed their diets to include fresh chicken, fish, whole grains, and vegetables.

I saw alcoholics and heroin addicts get clean and an elderly woman rise from a wheelchair. The healings seemed to be turning things around for so many people. We were a great success. During this time Mauro and Connie began an affair, just as I'd thought, and he moved out of Grandma Irene's to be with her. They were together constantly, and they worked well together during the night-time ceremonies.

The Anishnaabek told me about their childhoods: They had been taken from their families, placed in residential schools, and beaten for speaking their own language. Many had been subjected to police brutality. Some had seen friends and family killed. They told me of their grandparents and great-grandparents and how they had once lived off the land by trapping, hunting, fishing, and gathering wild foods. Now drug addiction and alcoholism were rampant. Suicides, murders, and car wrecks were among the leading causes of death in Manitoulin. I prayed with the Elders in front of pictures of people who'd recently died.

Carlos and I visited many homes, mostly poor, with children, elders, and grandparents living together in small clapboard houses. Some of the Anishnaabek hated whites, but because I was with Carlos I was invited into their homes.

One day we were called to a house on the Reserve. A Native woman named Kitty, an activist for Native people's rights, was wheelchair-bound, apparently from hysterical paralysis: She told us that she had asked God to give her the greatest suffering, to take on the pain of her people. She claimed that one day when her faith was strong enough she would be able to rise from the chair.

She had summoned us because she had a porcupine quill coming out of her chest. It hurt and she couldn't cover it with her blouse without the thing poking through the shirt's material. Carlos and I saw the quill traveling through her rib cage to her insides. It was easing out from inside her chest!

"This kind of thing happens in the Amazon," Carlos said. "Occasionally, a needle will pass through the sole of the foot. It can travel for years in the body until eventually it works its way out. The biggest danger is if it travels through the bloodstream and lodges in the heart."

This oddity was not at all strange to him. But to me, it was symbolic of the hopelessness and defeat that I saw in the community. People on the Reserve had been brutalized by the outside world, and now they were being stabbed from the inside out. The porcupine quill had found its way dangerously deep inside them, and it had festered for years. For generations! Getting it out was painful. Trying to cover it up was useless. Carlos and I were loosening the thorn, trying to free it and give the people a chance to heal.

As Carlos tried to remove the sharp quill that had broken through muscle and skin, we talked of witchcraft.

"A medicine man from the Yukon who was here helping our people ran into a tree on an empty road one night," Kitty told us. "The holy man hadn't been drinking. He died instantly. Then there was a nurse who was a very powerful medicine woman. She shot herself accidentally. Found in her possession was a ball of stuff that witches use to harm people."

"We Shuar call it *moosepa tsensak*, or *magica negra* in Spanish," Carlos said. "You're infected," he told Kitty. "I think it's best if you go to Wiki to have the quill removed surgically and get antibiotics."

After we left Kitty, Carlos and I went to our last ceremony. Before it began, Carlos gave a searing speech about the Anishnaabek's forefathers. "Your people were great strong warriors who fearlessly rode horseback on the plains. The bravest were your people, and this you must be once again. Do you think your braves were weak and sickly? Look how you have become so sick and dependent on Western handouts.

"Yes, you have been greatly oppressed, but now it is time for you to stand up and fight! Fight for your beliefs. Fight for your lives."

Carlos was a warrior and hero in the people's eyes. At his urging, with his help, they were getting stronger, braver, truer to their natures. Their happiness served us well. Carlos, Mauro, and I felt immense gratitude and love from the people we served.

Before we took the medicine that night, we were presented with gifts in a formal ceremony. Carlos received a purple satin jacket and Mauro a powwow shirt. I was given a traditional skirt patterned with flying eagles and pine trees. Colored ribbons ran along the hem.

Carlos turned to me and said, *"El Nation se acabó*. It's finished. If the people do not heal their sickness, the entire Nation will disappear."

CHAPTER THIRTY-TWO

The Bust

We'd had such great success that the Elders and the Wiki Council asked us to stay on and continue the healings. Carlos wanted to stay, but he was low on medicine and would have to go to Ecuador for more. He promised to return in a few weeks. I flew back to New York to see my daughter, and Mauro stayed on in Canada with Connie. We all planned to meet up again in Wiki in October.

Carlos was back in Canada in mid-October, but I stayed a week longer in New York because Manon had a semester break from school and I wanted to be with her. Carlos began healings on his own, with Mauro and Connie assisting. That's when all hell broke loose.

It was late afternoon, gray and cold in New York, the third week in October, when the phone rang. Carlos was on the other end, calling from Grandma Irene's. His voice poured out in a confusing jumble.

"She died. Everything was going along fine and—"

"Who died?"

"Last night during the ceremony," he said all in a rush. I could tell he was badly shaken. "Connie called me into the bathroom. An old woman named Janice had collapsed. I tried to revive her. I was giving her mouth-to-mouth. Connie called 911 and the ambulance came to take her away. She was breathing when they arrived, but just barely. The police came around two in the morning and asked Mauro and me questions. We were still in ceremony."

"What did they ask you?"

"They just asked if everything was all right, and they told us the woman had been taken to the hospital. I was relieved that she was being taken care of. The police were very nice and said they wouldn't disturb us any longer. Then they left.

"I said to everyone that we would stop the ceremony, but Janice's husband and son insisted we continue. Everyone prayed for Janice until morning came. We finished up, and Janice's husband and son came and hugged me. They were happy even though they were crying. They thanked me and told me I did nothing wrong. They wanted me to know they did not blame me for what had happened to her."

"How did she die, Carlos?"

"I found out this morning that she died on the way to the hospital. She had heart problems, and she was very sick. You know, Margarita, how sick so many of them are?"

"I know, Carlos. How many people were at the ceremony?"

"It was big. Around seventy people."

"What!"

I was dismayed to hear how many people had been there. I trusted myself to keep track of everyone, but who else was equipped to do it when I wasn't there? Seventy people? *That was way too many,* I thought. I would never have allowed Carlos to conduct a ceremony with that many people.

"Her heart gave out," Carlos went on. "She had diabetes. Tom, her husband, said that she'd gone to her doctor that day, and the doctor wanted her to go into the hospital. Tom and the boy said they were proud of my work and I had nothing to worry about. They said that Janice had told them she'd rather die in ceremony than die in a hospital. I didn't know she was going to die. I knew she was very sick, but there were so many people that night. Janice didn't even drink ayahuasca. 'No,' I told her. 'You won't take the medicine tonight.'"

I tried to interject, but Carlos kept on with the story. "Then the police came to Grandma's house, looking to talk to us some more. They wanted to know things about the ceremony and everything about Janice. I was completely honest—I'm a man of honor—and answered all their questions,"

"Carlos, you must be careful now what you tell me over the phone," I said. "I don't trust them."

"Mauro and I were taken into the station house this morning for questioning by the Ontario Provincial and tribal police."

"Did they take your passports?"

"No, but they've asked us not to have ceremonies until things are sorted out. They said Mauro and I could leave anytime we wanted. They said everything was fine and that we shouldn't worry."

But I was plenty worried. "Carlos, go back to Ecuador," I said. "Go back on the first flight."

"I am a warrior," he retorted. "I will not back down. What I do is holy work. I must stay and defend the sacred medicine."

"You are a warrior, but you need to leave Canada now." I felt it strongly in my gut—something bad was going to happen. I thought about how easy it had been for Carlos to get free of the police in Ecuador because his culture believed in aboriginal healing. But this wasn't Ecuador. I didn't think Carlos realized how dramatically the situation had changed. His mind-set was still the same, and it would not help him in North America.

Carlos stayed with Grandma Irene, whom he'd taken to calling Mama. We talked on the phone frequently. He hadn't been charged, and it began to look like everything was sorting itself out. I made plans to fly up so we could continue ceremonies. But a couple of days before I was to go, I got another call.

"Margarita, the police came with four patrol cars to arrest Mauro and me," Carlos said. "They had their guns out. They treated us like criminals. They seized the ayahuasca sitting on Grandma Irene's altar and demanded our passports. We went and got them. 'Why are you doing this?' I said, but they didn't answer.

"We were in jail for three days before Mama could get us out. The guards vaccinated us, and we both got so sick. I begged them not to give us the shot, because we'd never had anything like that in our systems before. I told them we were pure—spiritual men who could not have this bad medicine inside us. We both had high fevers and could not eat. We were freezing. I thought we would die in jail.

"Margarita, please come. I need you."

"I'll be there as soon as I can," I promised. "I'll find you a lawyer. We'll get through this."

But I wasn't convinced it would be that simple. He was now in the system and he had no passport to get home.

In late November, Carlos was arraigned and charged with multiple felonies: administering a noxious substance; importing a controlled substance into Canada; trafficking a controlled substance; possession of a controlled substance; criminal negligence causing death.

I flew to Canada to act as Carlos's translator at his bail hearing in mid-December. The courthouse was filled with angry protesters. The First Nation People wanted him released.

Carlos challenged the Crown to bring the sick into the courtroom: "In front of the tribunal, in front of the judge, deliver those who are sick. These I will heal. The Great Spirit is in me. There is no doubt, Carlos can speak clear.

"The plants of power are not mine. They are for everyone. For this I will fight with everything that is within me."

It was bizarre to see Carlos and Mauro, Amazonian Indians, in a courtroom in snowy Canada that followed the British system of justice. The judge wore a powdered wig. Every time I looked at him, I thought of angry crowds shouting, "Off with their heads!"

Carlos and I were seated together as I translated for him and the judge. Behind us sat a medicine man who we'd been told had been out to destroy Carlos with witchcraft. I suspected he had had a hand in Carlos's arrest as well. I remembered what Kitty had told us about the mysterious deaths of the medicine man and woman, and I heard there had been other deaths as well. Other healers had been killed and no one was ever caught. Grandma Irene told me that no medicine men in all of Canada or Alaska would set foot in Wiki.

"Then why did you let Carlos come?" I asked.

"We thought it would be okay, him being from South America. I never would have asked him and Mauro to come if I thought this would happen."

People were whispering in the courtroom as the judge deliberated. That man accused of sorcery sat behind us while we waited. Finally, bail was set, and a Manitoulin woman guaranteed her house for Carlos's and Mauro's release. Carlos was carried out of the courtroom to a chorus of cheers.

On our way to a diner where we were going to have lunch, I talked with his lawyer, a top-notch Toronto-based advocate on retainer, whose fees were astronomical. "It's going to be a tough battle," the lawyer said. "It will take a lot of money and maybe years to get this settled."

I was sitting in the restaurant when an Anishnaabek approached me. "The police are on their way to take you to the station for questioning," he said. "They are probably going to issue a warrant for your arrest."

Carlos and I exchanged a look of alarm. Just as a patrol car pulled into the parking lot, the Indians whisked me out the back door and took me into hiding. We met up at Grandma Irene's to quickly say good-bye and gather my things.

In the middle of the night, the Indians drove me 250 miles to Toronto, where I caught a train bound for New York. I was scurrying out of Canada, terrified that I would be nabbed at the border, but I got through.

CHAPTER THIRTY-THREE

Running Naked in Toronto

When I got back home, I started making calls to raise money to help Carlos and Mauro. But the people whom Carlos had healed in New York refused to help him with his legal fees. They refused even to acknowledge that they knew him! They were afraid the government would find out that they had used ayahuasca. I was horrified at their response, and Carlos didn't understand. How could they turn on and off like that? Meanwhile, the Native Americans began holding bingo games in Wiki, where they quickly raised three hundred dollars for a defense fund. After the police told them bingo was illegal, they had bake-offs.

Carlos wanted me to stay in Canada to be with him, but I couldn't for fear of being jailed. The pain of it seared me. I missed Carlos, and I did everything in my power to help him from New York. I was deeply sad and disturbed. What had happened? Where had things gone wrong?

Carlos and Mauro were placed under house arrest at Grandma Irene's. "My roots are cut," Carlos wept. "I am pressed down in a bottleneck. I have no money. I don't speak English. I am completely disconnected." He clung to me as his only connection to the world he knew. "Give the truth to others and write these words in my name, Margarita. Send a message to my people and ask for their help."

It seemed that Carlos and Mauro might languish under house arrest interminably. Carlos's cause became a cause celèbre among Native peoples—a focus of controversy about their right to choose their own methods of healing. Reportage on one of the hearings and its aftermath set the case within this context. One reporter wrote eighteen months after Janice's death:

> The wake of those tragic events on that mid-October evening in Wikwemikong...has left both a deep sadness and a division on the preferred fate of indigenous traditional healing practices, in both the Native and non-Native communities.

> Unlike the divisions that have occurred in the past, these new divisions are based on philosophy and beliefs in the efficacy of and right to choose one's own path of healing.

> That Native healing medicines do work is borne out clearly in the frantic efforts of huge multinational pharmaceutical companies, companies who are racing pell-mell to isolate and patent the active ingredients in traditional medicines for profit.

> In the aftermath of the death of Mrs. M., both the Shuar Amazonians and the M. family have come under threat and angry recrimination from supporters (and detractors on each side), actions that both the Shuar healers and Mrs. M. herself would doubtless decry.

During this time, I visited Canada several times in secret. I stayed off the streets because I was told the authorities were on the lookout for me. Grandma Irene was furious that Carlos and Mauro, whom she considered her sons, were still not free. "The

Anishnaabek are being punished by the Crown in Ontario," she said. "The police confiscated the holy vine and came into my home. The tribal police entered when I was not here. Meanwhile, all the people that Carlos and Mauro helped, they are getting sick again. Their treatments were not complete. We want our healers back. We want to get well, and we want them to be allowed to go home."

During one of my visits, Mauro and I talked frankly. It had been many months since he and Carlos were first charged and they still did not have a trial date. Mauro looked tired, defeated, and listless. Although he'd been recording songs to keep himself active, he didn't have the young, formidable face I'd seen in Ecuador. His intensity had been tempered by loss of freedom. He'd become depressed and had dreams that he was going to die, never to go back to his beloved Ecuador again.

We cried together. I felt so helpless with him. Carlos cried too, but somehow he was better at taking the punishment. I knew it was terribly hard for Carlos, but for Mauro to be under house arrest at his age, confined and facing the threat of jail at any moment, with the future so uncertain, was downright criminal.

"It's been a long time for me," Mauro admitted. At twenty-one years old, it must have felt like forever. "When I first came here I imagined sharing great things with the Indians. In Ecuador I thought that Indians lived in teepees. That's how naïve I was."

I asked him if he considered himself an uwishin.

"I was initiated on the path by my father and grandfather but I don't call myself uwishin," he replied.

"Well, what is an uwishin?" I asked him.

"An uwishin is a man who knows life, what life is. To be an uwishin is to know oneself. It is to know how to live. It is neither good nor bad. I do know the medicine and its value. I will give of myself so that the knowledge won't be lost. I will continue practicing and bring the truth wherever I go."

"What about being stuck here in Canada?"

"It is hard for my body. I'm not used to the food and snow and cold. There is always tension and stress in my mind."

"And your family?"

"I have not seen my wife and son for almost two years. It's as if my heart were put down and someone smashed it with a hammer. Everything has shattered into pieces." Even his affair with Connie didn't make up for the loss of his family, though she was now six months pregnant with his child. "But when someone has pain, you help them. That is why I came here with Papa, and when those we healed said, 'I feel good, the pain is gone,' I felt happy. I've come to learn that if you have pain in your heart, you pray to the Great Spirit that you can accept your life."

I assured Carlos and Mauro that I was doing everything possible in the States to help their cause. What I didn't tell them was that things seemed hopeless. I made great efforts to raise money for lawyers (not successfully) and get letters of commendation for their healing work that would be presented to the court. I desperately wanted Carlos and Mauro to be able to go back to Ecuador. After all, I had brought them up North. But I felt inept in the face of such difficulty. I'd spoken to Carlos's and Mauro's lawyers; they each had one now. The lawyers said that the trial might not begin until 2008 and could take years, not to mention several million dollars.

In October 1999, well before I met Carlos, before I knew that I would ever go to the Amazon, I had a vivid dream, and I wrote it down. There in Canada, I pulled out my journal and read again what I had written.

I am in a misty jungle; the trunks and branches of trees, leaves, vines enwrap me. Parrots alight on my arm to be petted. A ring of small deer and pacas surrounds me. It's quiet—a muted paradise. I lie by a green pool, letting my arm drop lazily into the water. My body begins to vibrate softly. Then I am climbing trees. I am a large cat, moving through a tangle of greens, luscious and wet. I smell the moistness and humus of the earth.

The sunlight bleeds through the canopy as a black jaguar comes upon me, purring in a haunting, trancelike rhythm. We run together through the forest. I am a sleek and spotted golden jaguar. The short fur ripples over my shoulders as my paws fly over the matted leaves on the ground. I pant and cough, my head swinging from side to side. I am lying next to the black jaguar, being licked by a salty and broad tongue that cleanses my solar plexus and my breast. Licking. Soothing. Safe. My chest rises and my heart speeds up. A powerful black beast: my mentor.

Then a zipper splits open and the illusion breaks. The black jaguar runs and suddenly transforms into a dark-skinned Indian. He is running naked as fast as he can through the streets of Toronto, fleeing the police.

I flew back to the States after a tearful good-bye. In Canada it was impossible for me to work with Carlos. By court order, he was not even allowed to give massages! I could study with him no longer.

The great healing work we were destined to do together—the glory that we'd envisioned, prayed for, and hoped for, and that briefly came to pass—had been blown away like dust. Carlos and I had come to a crashing end. I never received the flechas.

Epilogue

I was finally able to free Carlos and Mauro in late January of 2003. I traveled to Ecuador with Grandma Irene, where we gave television and radio interviews, made a personal plea to the vice president, and convinced the Ecuadorian government to pressure the Canadians.

The case in Canada was concluded forty-eight hours after the pretrial hearing in spring of that year. Mauro was allowed to go home right away. In the Wiki courthouse the Crown noted Carlos's sincerity and acknowledged a notebook of glowing testimonials from people he had healed. He was convicted of using the "noxious substance" tobacco and sentenced to six months of community service in Manitoulin.

When Carlos returned to Ecuador, Mauro was dealing with hardships that two years in Canada had wrought. After the extended separation, he and his wife were fighting. Eventually he began writing and recording music with a group of his schoolmates. He was never able to go back to Canada to see his child with Connie.

Carlos resumed his family life with his common-law wife and children. He offered his full powers of healing to the community and treated locals whether they had money or not. His response as an aboriginal to the accolades and wealth of my country was, I came to realize, not all that unusual. He hadn't acted differently than other indigenous healers who've come to America. Thankfully, all the money and acclaim hadn't damaged his healing abilities. But I don't think I will ever understand what America represents to indigenous people.

Carlos claimed that the Great Spirit held him in Canada to defend the medicine and to impose rest on his body after thirty-five years of nonstop healing. He never admitted to any misjudgment. He began work on a clinic in Ecuador, with backing from the Anishnaabek in Canada. Grandma Irene went on to head ASIMI, the Anishnaabek Support of Indigenous Medicine, an international agency.

Manon went to college, became a concert pianist, and enrolled in graduate school in New York City. Miles continued making magnificent films, and in time he remarried.

I have no regrets for myself, although I would wish that Carlos and Mauro had not had almost three years taken from them. After what happened in Canada, I could have been hardened. Instead, I chose to see my lessons as an opportunity to keep opening, to keep exploring, to live more consciously and lovingly.

Carlos taught me to clearly and willfully function when I was in the grip of the medicine and bombarded by visions. He taught me to assume the stance of the warrior, to get "sober." And I came to realize that the purpose of my work with him was to be able to bring that balance into daily life, in our everyday human interactions.

There is much for *all* of us to learn in the tradition that Carlos embodies. The worlds of Spirit and Nature through which he moves so fluidly and with such authority are part of our common heritage.

I believe it is a terrible mistake to think that they have somehow been supplanted by our technological superiority, our organized religion, or the belief that we have evolved beyond our ancestors. I came to know from my odyssey into the jungle that ancient and so-called primitive cultures saw a close relationship between the act of love and the act of creation. Knowledge of vital import flows from the depths of each one of us. The experience of my illness taught me that when we are in crisis we must often walk through fire; it taught me that there is another world full of possibility and promise beyond fear. It is the world of healing and true growth for which so many of us yearn.

Through my journeys with Carlos, I learned that I am willing to risk everything for what I know is true and good. I learned that I am able to endure almost anything—purgings, terrors, privations. I learned that in ceremony, I am complete. Connected. Alive. Ayahuasca gave me insight into the hidden, masked aspects of myself, and that self-discovery led to my healing. I have learned that in order to be true to myself I must keep on doggedly uncovering parts of myself that are hidden and trapped. This process continues: It is never done. I continue to explore the part of me that lives in the spiritual realm and is a conduit of spirit, capable of miraculous healing.

Carlos taught me to create a balanced spirituality within myself. I have been able to harmonize my life with larger, more universal values reflecting the Great Spirit. I have been able to cultivate awareness, compassion, empathy, and loving regard for all life. I have been able to help others heal as divine spirit works through me.

With his vast and luminous resources, Carlos *is* one of the greatest healers alive today. He showed me remarkable treatments that were both death-defying and life-affirming, and I know what he is capable of. I have an abiding love for him—forever—as he does for me. I owe him my life, but I owe him more than that. Carlos fully empowered me. He took me by the hand and led me into the sacred territory that I now inhabit.

After his return to Ecuador in 2003, I could have studied with him in his homeland, gone through the full initiation and received the flechas, but so much time had passed and our work together had come to a natural conclusion. Carlos is my friend, companion, teacher, and once-lover. I know whenever I need him, or he needs my help, we will come to each other's aid.

I continue walking on the Red Path with the wisdom Carlos passed on to me. I have been fortunate to have formidable spirits accompany me as I travel to Brazil and Africa to study with other healers of great capacity…but that is another story.

Acknowledgments

I am humbly grateful to Carlos and the ayahuasca spirit for their love and teachings.

To David Nelson, my editor at Sterling, I wish to express sincere thanks for having worked so diligently with me and with unwavering faith in *Black Smoke*. I am grateful for his friendship, encouragement, and commitment. I wish to acknowledge Anne Barthel and Hannah Reich for their special talent, generosity, and love of both language and healing. Their astuteness and skill helped make this project a success. I'd also like to thank Tracy Brown, Patty Gift, Steve Magnuson, Philip Turner, Kenneth Wapner, and the staff at Sterling for their inspiring support and hard work in helping me put this book together.

A special thanks goes to my dear friend Jeanne Fleming for encouraging me through this enormous project. She was there during the brightest moments and the very stormy periods of this book's birth. Her incisive brilliance, love, and generosity guided me in developing my work. I'd like to thank her saintly husband, Harlan Matthews, for keeping my car running.

To Manon, for being born. I love you unconditionally. To my ex-husband for being a fantastic father to our daughter and for supporting me while I wrote this book. To Michael Lukeson, whose inspiration and love continue to surprise me. Thank you to my family: Bowen Daniel, Yvonne Daniel, Brad Daniel, and Lottie May Kipp. To my dearest sisters: Ann Patty, Susan Quasha, Susan Moran, Susan Ray, Josie RavenWing, Lara Chkhetiani, Gina Rabbin, Chie Hammons, Cynthia Beatt, A.A. Parker, Lilli Farrell, Patty Cowan, Erin Schulman, Wendy Ewald, and Kiki Smith. And a big thank you to Tom McDonough, Burrill Crohn, and Rudy Wurlitzer.

Finally, I would like to thank the many wonderful Ecuadorians who befriended me in Morona Santiago, Imbabura Province, and Tumbaco. And even though I cannot name you, I am ever grateful to the First Nation people in Canada.

About the Author

Margaret De Wys is a composer and faculty member at the Milton Avery Graduate School of the Arts. A dramatic shift in her life set her on a pilgrimage to Ecuador and to becoming a world traveler and explorer dedicated to the preservation and transmission of traditional wisdom in the modern world. She currently divides her time between Upstate New York and Southeast Nigeria.